Motivating Kids

Ronit Baras

National Library of Australia

Cataloguing -in-publication- data

Baras Ronit 2019

Motivating Kids

ISBN 9781537427850

1. English Non fiction 2. Parenting 3. Education 4. Motivation (psychology)

To order books please contact:

Be Happy in LIFE
12 Chelva Street
Wishart, QLD, 4122
Australia

Phone: +61 7 33432237

Email: books@behappyinlife.com

Website: www.behappyinlife.com/books

Editor: Dr. Tina Riveros

Cover design: Mudskipper Design, Sandy Lokas/Edenhall Studio

Be the change you want to see in the world

– Mahatma Gandhi

TABLE OF CONTENTS

ABOUT THE AUTHOR

Ronit Baras is an educator, life coach, author, journalist, justice of peace and motivational speaker. She has been coaching and teaching emotional intelligence techniques for over 30 years in several countries (USA, Israel, Thailand, Singapore & Australia). She has developed and implemented many educational programs for teachers, parents and children, which have been hugely successful.

Ronit is the founder and director of Be Happy in LIFE. She is teaching at the University of Queensland and a trainer for the institute of public administrators (IPAA) Queensland, is the State Director of Together for Humanity Foundation, was the school's program director of the Global Learning Centre and has conducted many relationship and parenting workshops around the world.

Through her presentations and writing Ronit delivers inspiring messages of love, respect, acceptance, motivation and determination.

Ronit has helped many parents around the world establish great relationships with their kids and discover the joys of successful and mindful parenting. She has been teaching, coaching, presenting and writing over 30 years and her educational writing has appeared in educational magazines around the world. Her blog, Family Matters (www.ronitbaras.com), is a great practical resource for parents and teachers, already containing over 1600 articles on personal development, education, relationships, family life and parenting. With her writing, she has touched the lives of millions of readers from around the world.

Ronit thinks that people can (and should) live a happy life by learning basic emotional skills to manage their feelings and actions and to take charge of their life and that parents are best to pass on those skills to their children.

Ronit believes that *"Parents are very important agents of their children's identity. To support their kids' development, they need to be able to support themselves and have basic motivation skills. Parenting requires high emotional intelligence, which is the key to success in life. If we want to raise a generation of happy and motivated kids, we need to focus on teaching them happiness and motivation. Luckily, happiness and motivation can be developed. They are the key for opening the doors to endless possibilities"*.

I often hear the question *"How do you motivate kids to do things?"* Most parents in the world would like to know the "magic tricks" of motivating their kids to succeed, to be friendly, healthy and happy. I guess it is part of having kids, that desire for them to be "in the zone", where everything is easy and gives a good feeling. In this sense, kids and their parents are exactly the same. Kids need motivation and parents need motivation. **Motivation has no age and this book will cater to both parents and kids.**

In my parenting classes, 100% of the participants want their kids to have love, success, friendships, confidence and happiness. All parents look for the formula to help their kids get these things.

In this book, I will share with you all there is to know about motivating your kids. This **ultimate guide** to motivation is based on more than 30 years of education experience and practical work around the world with parents, teachers and kids of all ages. I have perfected this tool kit over the years by researching its effectiveness with parents, kids and readers. I am happy and delighted to share them with you as well. In this book, I cover all aspects of motivations and how you, as a parent, can use each and every one of them to give your kids what you have always wanted – motivate them to be the best they can be.

During many years of work, coaching and seeing thousands of parents and children, I realized that reading/hearing about motivation is not enough. We all read a great book, say, "Tomorrow, I will do things differently", and after three days, we go back to old habits. I don't want this book to be another one of those wonderful books that slip out of the mind three days later.

I value theory and research, but they don't stand the tests of reality. People understand things pretty quickly, but they are always left with *"Ok, what do I do with this knowledge and how do I do it?"* which only increases the feeling of frustration and inadequacy. They know what they don't know and can't do anything about it.

This is why I made the decision early in my career that action and practical tools are much more powerful than just theory and I have dedicated much of my energy to build a tool kit that my clients can actually use to get what they want.

This book is not only about the "Why?" but also the "how to?" and in the simplest way. I wanted every parent to be able to implement those techniques in a very easy way without having to go through a degree studying psychology or education. I have included tips and practical tools that when you try them, you are guaranteed to get results. Over the years, I have had millions of clients and readers and many fans raving about this approach. I have had many people leave a workshop then sending me an email that night saying *"I am shocked. I got home and it worked straight away"* or readers sending me emails to share their successful use of those tips and tools. I promise it'll do the same for you.

So, how can you use the book?

In each chapter, I have included tips, exercises and/or printable resources to help you on this exciting mission. Let's not forget, I am an educator and highly believe in practice and homework. Think of it as a personal, private course in motivation that you can do at your own pace that will get you great results. I encourage you to try all the exercises in this book. I have managed to help thousands of families by choosing single activities from my tool kit that suits their needs. You can imagine the impact of using all of them.

At the end of each chapter, you will find a summary of all the important things covered in the chapter. The summaries are practical and include suggestions and tips. They will mean more to you after you read the chapters and mean even more when you complete at least some of the activities suggested.

The last chapter is a summary of all chapters' summaries and is a good refresher once you have completed the book and become your kids' motivational parent. Use the last summary as a reminder and examine your progress every three month. Remember, motivating your kids is a skill you need to develop if you want to help them to be happy, healthy and successful in life.

Throughout the book, I've included names of blog posts with more information. To find them, visit www.ronitbaras.com and search for their name.

I wish you exciting and practical reading and I hope you'll make good use of this new knowledge to motivate yourself and your own kids.

Remember, happy parents raise happy kids.

Ronit

PARENTING, COACHING AND MOTIVATION

Parents are the most important agents of their kids' life. They are the first and most crucial source of information and the main reference for their kids' identity. Big words, it means that you, yes, you, if you are a parent, have an important job, important and with lots of responsibility. If it seems too heavy to carry, it is also the most enjoyable and exciting journey you will ever take.

Bringing kids into this world is a selfish act. Yes, I know most people cringe at this point, but think about it, you brought your kids to life for you, not for them. They did not exist when you made your decision to have them.

With this mentality (which I believe we all have), it is hard to parent kids, because it is all about us and not about them. The best parenting is when the kids' best interest is the main concern. You see, this is why when couples go through separation or divorce, their main challenge is to find the balance between the kids' best interest and theirs. None of them can be neglected. As I have covered in my parenting program, Happy Parents Raise Happy Kids, I believe that for parents to do a good parenting job, they need to take care of themselves too.

There are many challenges in parenting and many parents are in pursuit of rules for establishing and maintaining a happy family. There are many systems to follow, many books to read, many rules to examine, much research to read, a lot of advice to listen to and many mistakes to make and I believe that each parent must find his or her own magic formula. Yes, read a lot, listen a lot, experience a lot, succeed, fail and make your own choices: the choices that are good for you as a parent. The magic about success is that you know you have reached it only when you reach it, but when you get there, you have no doubts.

Over 30 years of work with kids and families, I have found that being your kids' life coach is the most successful, efficient and practical parenting system.

A life coach is a person empowering people to be what they want to be. It is a person who helps clients grow, evolve and help facilitate change. Though life coaching is a very new trendy name for "personal development", it has been in practice for hundreds of years. At first it was the role of the elders and slowly, over years transferred to the educators and lately become a field associated with psychology and motivational speakers. I have been a life coach for over 30 years and used it in many areas of life and I can tell you that the system works magic with children, especially if they are your children.

 Your children will become what you are; so be what you want them to be

– David Bly

Here are some of the rules of coaching that can be 100% applicable in parenting.

1. In coaching, **the coach must constantly work on his or her emotional state**. You cannot possibly give when you do not have enough. If you are a parent and want happy kids, make sure you are happy.

2. In coaching, **the coach can only give (not force) and the client must take**. In parenting, you cannot force kids to do things (well, yes, you can, but it is only temporary, because it only teaches your kids that you have more power and that strong people abuse their power over others, which kills one of the most important qualities in people – trust!) Parents can only give kids the tools and kids must be able to take them and use them.

3. In coaching, **both coach and client agree to respect each other**. They never call each other names, they appreciate each other's time, they are grateful, and they listen and care for each other. In parenting, this is essential. Respectful parents raise respectful kids.

4. In coaching, the whole relationship is **based on targets**. The client sets the goals and the coach helps him or her reach them. In parenting, we need to help our kids set goals for themselves and we help them achieve them. The more we do this, the more focused our kids will be and the happier.

5. In coaching, **there is no "one size fits all" philosophy**. What is good for one might be too tight for others. A good coaching program is tailored. In parenting, there is no point using the same techniques your parents have used or what worked for you with older children. No two kids are the same,

so if you try something and it does not work, be flexible and try something else.

6. In coaching, **the coach must keep their own agenda aside and focus on the clients' needs**. As I said, this is one of the biggest challenges of coaches and parents. In parenting, we need to do the same. Remember, when you are parenting it is not about you but about your kid. If you are working too hard, you are probably in the wrong "zone" and you are trying to make your kid fit into your parenting style instead of adjusting your style to theirs. When your agenda is more important, be clear about it so everyone knows it is about you.

7. In coaching, **the coach is there to encourage and support the client every step of the way**. Support means 100%. In parenting, we need to give 100% support in the form of unconditional love. It is not punishment when kids do not follow our rules but encouragement when things do follow our own rules. Focusing on the positive is one of the coach's most important tools. Parents should use it too.

8. In coaching, **the coach helps the client find the motivation inside instead of being subject to external pressure**. Parents are a great pressure point in their kids' life. We need to teach our children to find reasons within to do things. If they do things for us, it will not last forever. Motivation is like a muscle. If kids learn to use it, they can motivate themselves to do anything. If they do it for other's approval and acceptance, they will end up grownups that are dependent on others' approval and acceptance. This is a formula for trouble.

9. **The coach has a personal style but will present information in a way that suits the client**. A coach will never use his clients to duplicate himself in order to justify his own thoughts, philosophy or actions. Parents using this approach will have better results and better relationship with their kids. Parents and kids are different in age, style, personality, responsibility and many other aspects. If we went to help our kids find the best in themselves, we must accept and appreciate that our kids are different. Some kids are better at some skills and others have challenges, if they are not like us, there is nothing wrong with them. They are not an extension of us; they are unique individuals living their uniqueness.

10. In coaching, **the coach talks about their own challenges and offers solutions but is very clear that it is the client's choice what to do with that information**. In parenting, if we talk about our success and challenges, about our childhood and friends with honesty, it helps our kids realize that we are human and that their journey in life is just natural. It can inspire and motivate them to never give up and keep moving forward and can build

their resilience but when we share, we give our kids the choice what to do with that information.

11.   In coaching, **the client's success is the coach's success**. In parenting, it is the same. When our children succeed, we walk around like peacocks and proud as if we had something to do with that (which we did). Help your kids succeed, their success is yours.

"*Success is not final, failure is not total. It is the courage to continue that counts*" - *Winston Churchill*

© *www.ronitbaras.com*

Tips for becoming your kids' coach

✓   Assess if you are using a coach mentality in order to help your kids, guide or motivate them to do things.

✓   When kids are young, they talk lots, ask questions, giggle and make noises. As they grow, the balance between who does the talking changes. At the end of the day go over all your communication with your child and ask yourself "Who did most of the talking?" If you are the coach, the child is doing most of the talking.

✓   Adopt the "kind listener" mentality. There are four states of listening, kind listener, empathic, critical and problem solver. Though we sometimes need to be a critical or problem solver parent, we must start with being kind and clearing the space for the speaker without judgment and without asking the question "what does it mean about me?" Coaching mentality requires kindness. Assess your communication with your child and ask yourself in which listening mode are you? Aim for kindness.

✓ Make sure you have goals and teach your kids to work with goals and targets. Living by model is the best thing.

✓ Every time you lose your temper, you cannot coach/ parent because it is a sign you are not in control. When you are not in control, let go of your coaching desire, arrange your thoughts and feelings and try again when you are calm and cool. Why? Because kids have sensors, they can tell you are not in control and they can't be inspired or motivated to do what you want them to do.

✓ Games are a wonderful tool of every coach and essential for every parent. I covered the topic of using games as a learning tool in my thesis as a wonderful motivator.

Here is a brief description of the importance of games in any learning process and why it is a wonderful motivating tool.

Children play games for many purposes. For example, games can be used to improve social skills. During games, kids must negotiate, share, relate and connect with others. This helps develop understanding, compassion, empathy, acceptance and trust, and later on, allows healthy intimacy.

Games can be used to pass time, relax and feel calm. The repetition helps kids "predict" the future and gives them a sense of stability. The "fun" of the games triggers the release of chemicals that heal loneliness, anger, anxiety and depression and the completion of the game helps develop a sense of achievement.

 There is no point in being grown up if you can't be childish sometimes

– Dr. Who

Games can be used to learn. Games stimulate kids' imagination and curiosity, improve memory and develop persistence, perseverance and creativity. They help develop new skills, experiment with trial and error, learn problem-solving techniques and strengthen existing skills. Games require learning rules, following them and taking advantage of them to suit the needs of the participant, which is a handy skill that children require for success.

Above all, playing games is fun and enjoyable, which is one of the most motivating factors for learning in humans. Psychiatrist, researcher and writer Mihaly Csikszentmihalyi described play in his work *Flow, The Psychology of Optimal Experience* (1990) as a state of flow that requires just *"the right balance of challenge and opportunity"*. If the game is too hard or too easy, it loses its sense of pleasure and fun.

If you can, make every activity in this book a game. I do this in my coaching programs, my parenting workshops and even when I teach university students and it works magic because it takes advantage of the Fun Incentive.

Parenting is very much like life coaching. You can, if you want, be your kids' coach and have happy relationships in your family. With happy relationship, it is easy to motivate kids to do whatever you want.

Summary

✓ Parents are the best potential motivators as they are the most important agents of socialization.

✓ Parents and coaches are givers. The parent as a coach is the best approach in motivating children and directing them to a desired outcome. The Coaching relationship is personalized, focused, includes respect and is supportive and motivating.

✓ To allow motivation to happen, kids need to do most of the talking and parents have to be "kind listeners" and be in control of their own feelings.

✓ Games are a wonderful tool for learning. Use the "fun Incentive" to motivate your child.

2 CHAPTER TWO

MOTIVATION, SAILING AND WAR

To understand how motivation works it is important to understand how our conscious and subconscious works. The science of the brain function in motivation has been researched for many years and many theories regarding this have been put forward.

 It is not what you say out of your mouth that determines your mind, it's what you whisperer to yourself that has the most power

— Robert T. Kiyosaki

Over the years, teaching those theories to so many clients and students, I discovered that storytelling was very effective in understanding and remembering the science of the mind and as a result, I wrote the story "Sailing on the Ship of Life". In this story, I have included many of the theories into one story. This is my ship story. I hope you will be able to match it to real life.

Sailing on the Ship of Life

The Captain of the "I" ship stood at the helm of his ship looking at the horizon and holding the steering wheel. He was not very happy about the condition of his ship and the direction it was taking. They had been sailing for a long time without success.

Yet, every time he had talked to his crew about the poor condition of the "I" ship and told them he was not happy about where it was headed, the crew had calmly ignored his frustration.

"Captain", said the First Mate, "We have been working on this map for many years. Our job is to protect the ship from any harm, even if it means we need to protect it from you. We will not change course unless you convince us it is safe for the ship".

Sometimes, he felt he was not the Captain and that the crewmembers were making decisions by themselves. The captain of the "I" ship felt very frustrated. He stood at the helm, his parrot Max on his shoulder, and longed to experience success and comfort.

"A ship should not be in this condition", said Max the parrot, "Just look at any magazine or any TV show. There are wonderful ships there, looking young and fresh with lots of technology".

"Are you sure it is not all a façade, Max?" asked the Captain.

"No, Captain. They sail on easy waters, they have all the luxury they want and look at you, sailing a beaten old ship with a disobedient crew. Your parents had other plans for you and what will others say about you and your ragged ship?"

The Captain felt very bad about it. The more he imagined the papers, magazines and TV celebrity ships, the worse he felt. The thought of disappointing his family and showing himself in any ship gathering almost made him freak out.

"You don't have to listen to your crew", said Max.

"Maybe not, but I need them, you know", said the Captain.

"No, you don't. They are just a bunch of losers. What do they know? You are the Captain! You just tell them where to go and be firm and they will listen. You need to give orders and make sure you do it loudly enough for them to listen", said Max.

"You're right. Max. I'm the Captain here", said the Captain and called out, "Sail to the North, turn right 20 degrees". He tried very hard to steer his wheel to the right. The mighty "I" ship made a slight turn to the right.

"Well done, Captain", said Max, "You did it! I told you all you had to do was be firm and loud. Your crew will only respond to orders".

The Captain was very happy with the new direction, but after three days of holding his steering wheel tight, he felt very tired and went to rest. When he got up in the morning, he realized his ship was on the old course again. He felt very confused.

"This is impossible. Unheard of! What's wrong with you, Captain? You have no control over your ship", said Max.

"But I…" started the Captain.

"You might as well leave everything to the crew and jump overboard", said Max from the Captain's shoulder.

The Captain felt helpless.

"Well, what on Earth are you doing?" continued Max, "Get up and do something".

The Captain felt he was under pressure. He did not know what to do. He thought that holding onto the steering wheel for three days was hard enough. He looked around to find some support. His crewmembers seemed to be going back and forth moving things and looking busy. He was so humiliated by such an uncooperative crew.

"Are you happy?" he shouted to his crewmembers in frustration and tears formed in his eyes.

"Sorry, Captain. Our role is to protect the ship. What you may think will bring you happiness right now may risk the ship later. We can't afford to change course just because you watch too much TV and think that sailing North for a quick touch up job will make you happy. Trust us! It won't. If the timber is rotten, the ship needs a lot more than a touch up job", said the First Mate.

The Captain nearly cried. He had heard so much about the mechanic who fixed up ships on the North port. He looked around at his ragged ship. The oil was spilling, and sails were worn.

"Never mind", he said in despair and went to open a bottle of rum to ease the humiliation of his defeat.

The next two months were very tough for the Captain and his "I" ship. The ship went through storms and strong winds. The sails were torn and neither the captain nor the crew were able to direct the ship to shore. The captain, supported by his devoted parrot Max, comforted himself with solitude, food and rum.

Two months later, as The Captain looked at the horizon and the sun was shining, he told Max.

"What do you say Max? I really would like to sail north to see that ship fixer upper. Do you think I can hold onto the steering wheel long enough this time?"

"No", said Max.

"Why not?" asked the Captain in surprise.

"Because you're a loser. Look at your ship. You have never succeeded in doing anything like that. We have been through the same thing many times already. What makes you think you can do it this time?"

The Captain felt lonely. Even his devoted parrot had no faith in him.

"Well, Maybe I think I can do it because now I want it more than ever", he tried to convince Max, "Like in the saying 'Where there's a will there's a way'".

"How do you know that your will is strong enough this time? And does that mean that two month ago, it wasn't?" said Max sarcastically.

The Captain thought about it for a while. He did not know. Sometimes, when the sun shone bright, he had felt he was strong and able, but then again, last time he had the exact same feeling of discomfort and a desire to sail north. He had no way of knowing when his will was strong enough. He felt even more defeated. He could imagine himself sailing in the same old "I" ship on the same old course, not having a clue how to change.

"Just give it up, Captain", suggested Max.

The captain thought about it for a while. Maybe it is better to know your weaknesses and accept them. He will never have a beautiful, fully functional ship.

"Just accept it, Captain. You're a loser with no control over your ship", said Max.

The Captain went to his room feeling very depressed. He went to bed and turned on the TV. He felt sick. He will take time off from his captaincy. As he fell asleep, he heard max whispering.

"If I were you, I would jump overboard".

Did you know?

Research about goals found that only 10% of people live life with a sense of direction by setting themselves goals, while the rest float aimlessly. Aim to be one of the 10%. They happen to be the most successful people.

Three players in the game of life

If you have ever felt helpless, defeated and unhappy, just like the captain of the "I" ship, welcome to the real world! We are all sailing on the ocean of life: adult and children alike. We sail every day, with every decision and choice we make or reject. The water and the weather are unpredictable and to our aid come three important characters:

The **Captain** is our **conscious** mind – our ability to analyze and reason

The parrot **Max** is the **little voice** in our head – our self-talk, telling what we think

The **crew** is our **subconscious** mind – our hidden motives, feelings and ability to act quickly and intuitively

Understanding the "Self" – Captain and Crew

When you are unhappy, it means your captain decides to sail to the "right" and your crew sails to the "left". Your conscious and subconscious minds are not communicating.

Theories about human behavior claim that the conscious and subconscious have different roles in maintaining the ship's health, wealth and wellbeing.
Captains change over the years and their role is to direct the ship.
Crewmembers are there from day one and their role is to protect the ship from any harm and keep it safe.

Unfortunately, the crew holds more than 90% of the decision-making, while captains, who are highly influenced by Max and external sources, like media and what happened in the past, hold only 10% of the decision-making.

The Crew can only communicate with their ship's captain. The captain holds the key to the internal communication system with the crew and no one else can talk to the crew except the captain. The crew cannot communicate with anyone else but their captain and cannot be influenced by any other captain. Therefore, whenever you say, "*Someone else made me do that*", you are cheating yourself. No one can make you do anything. It is all a choice. Conscious or subconscious but still a choice. Your "captain" gave an order and your "crew" chose to obey. Do not blame anyone else for your ship's condition and do not expect anyone else to come and fix your ship. Life is a continuous sailing journey and only you can take care of the condition of your ship. If you want to help your kids, help them build a good communication channel between their captain and crew rather than telling them what to do. You talk to their captain, but they need to talk to their crew.

Generally, **Crewmembers do not like changes**. They need to go through lots of convincing before they change course. Even if you experience lots of pain from a course that is not healthy for their captain, like health problems, financial difficulties or relationship breakdowns and the captain thinks he knows why and wants to change it, the crew members will hold on to their plan and they will win. If you want to change your kids' behavior, beware, the crew doesn't like it. It is complicated to change yourself, do not be tempted to try to change your kids. Only they can do it and it requires skill and time.

Every time the captain wants to **change the course because of jealousy**, like wanting a big house just like the Jones's, to be slim like Barbie or wealthy like Richard Branson, the crew rejects it. They think the captain is not in control of the ship and highly manipulated by external sources. This usually presents a threat and a risk for the crew. In this mindset, captains are not fully responsible, so the crew takes over the wheel. Do not use the jealousy method to try to motivate your kids to do things. Avoid *"Be like your sister"* or *"look at Ben"* or *"Why can't you be like him?"* If your kids act on this jealousy, their crew will resist,
their feeling of inadequacy and lack of control will increase and no change will happen, because the crew will win.

Whenever the captain wants to change the course **to please another ship**, (and many young captain's desire is to please their parents' ship) the crewmembers treat this situation as **a threat**. They say, "*The Captain is not in his normal mind, he is under pressure, we need to protect him from himself. All engines stop, shields up, red alert!*" This is when the ship is stuck and not moving anywhere and every ship that gets too close is fired upon. If you want to change things in your life, make sure you are not under any pressure. If you want to change things in your kids' life, make sure they are not under any pressure. Pressure is a sign you are stuck, and the crew will throw anchors overboard until the "threat" disappears.

Some people are in this position for years, with anchors deep in the sand and they can't move, feeling stuck and helpless. The longer the anchors are in the ground, the harder it is for them to lift them and start sailing. It is the same with kids. The more pressure you put on them, the more stuck your kids will be.

Unfortunately, too many ships consider one or two of their parents a threat and this is why they have to stay away from them in order to have a happy life. You can read my blog post Divorcing Your Parents, and the poll inside it, to realize the magnitude of this phenomenon and make sure your kids will think differently about it. Kids cannot do things to please. It goes against their constitution. Their crew is much stronger.

Crewmembers do not accept any touch up orders. They think that when the ship's timber is rotten, there is no point covering it up with a coat of paint. It needs a carpenter. So, watch what you are trying to do. If it is temporary relief, your crew will undermine your efforts and may even throw you overboard. It is very important to pay attention to the maintenance long before it is rotten. It is similar to going to the dentist. You have to brush your teeth twice a day and floss and every six months go to the dentist for a checkup and cleaning. This is how you avoid root canal. You can't go to the dentist and say can you do a filling to cover up the rotten canal. If you have a problem, treat it immediately. If you have a conflict that keeps coming up, treat it immediately. If you gain weight, treat it immediately, if kids drop in their performance in school, treat it immediately before the timber starts rotting.

Crewmembers do not like negative orders. In fact, the crew will do the opposite of a negative command. If the captain says, *"I do not want a fat ship"*, the crew says, *"Fat ship! Aye, aye, Captain"* and puts some more weight on the ship. Captains must learn to say what they want and avoid saying what they do not want. It will keep the ship in a much better shape. Beautiful, healthy, wealthy ships have captains who are clear about what they want and look forward to a positive future. If you want to help your kids, make sure to use a positive language and teach them to talk in positive language as well so their crew will cooperate with them.

The crew needs a lot of convincing. If your will is not strong, they will question it until you give up. A persistent captain is the only captain who can make them accept a new course. **Most captains will hold a will for 3 days** (starting a diet, making an effort to change attitude or reading a book, trying to implement its suggestions or persisting with a new parenting technique). As soon as they let go, the crew sees that as a sign their will is not strong enough and reverses the changes. This is why it is very hard to make kids do things if they don't have a very strong will (and as we said, jealousy, pleasing mom and dad or fear of punishment cannot be translated into "strong will"). Your job as a parent is to help them develop a strong will of their own so they can easily convince their crew to change course.

If one does not know to which port one is sailing, no wind is favorable

– Seneca

The crew only works with goals. The problem that most captains have is sailing without knowing the destination. Research about goals found that only 10% of people live life with a sense of direction by setting themselves goals, while the rest float aimlessly. Think about it this way. You get off the airplane at the airport, get into a taxi and say nothing. The taxi driver will start the meter but wait until you tell him where to go. A taxi driver cannot take you to your destination if you don't tell him where to go. Life is the same; your ship's engine is on, using fuel, wasting lots of energy and your crew will wait until you tell them where to go.

The Roman philosopher Seneca said that people must know where they are going if they want to be able to use the circumstances to their advantage. You see, if you know where you are sailing to, instead of drifting during a storm, you can direct your sails so the wind will get to your destination **faster**. Life offers a variety of sun, wind and rain. Successful people do not have less sun, wind or rainbows. They just use them to their advantage.

If you teach your kids to have goals and to communicate them to the crew regularly, they will be in the 10% of successful people and it'll guarantee their crew will be more cooperative for years to come.

Crewmembers never accept vague goals. If the Captain says, *"Let's sail there"*, the crew will ask where exactly "there" is. And if the captain does not know for sure, the command is rejected immediately. The more specific the coordinates are, the more likely the crew is to follow your order. Saying *"I want to look good"* is not specific and so it is immediately classified as "wishful thinking" (over a long period, this creates a life of "wishful sinking").

Captains do not like being specific. They are afraid they might not get to the exact same coordinates they have set for themselves. Vague goals are a cop out. They allow for the possibility of not achieving.

If you want to achieve a career goal, be specific about the kind of work you are looking for, what the boss should be like, how much you want to be paid and how long you are willing to commute. If you want to achieve a financial goal, be specific about how much money you want, what you want it for and how long it will take you to get it. If you want to have amazing children for example, teach them to have specific and focused goals about their own character, their hobbies, their manner, skills and talents.

Aim for the moon. If you miss, you may hit a star

– W. Clement Stone

Crewmembers work with dates and calendars. Captains, for the same reason, prefer to be vague. They do not like to commit to a date and a time. They prefer to say, *"One day I will travel the world"*, *"Someday I will be healthy"*, *"In the future, I will have enough money to…"* which guarantees they will never get anywhere. We call it the "one day file". This is the file our crew possesses that becomes the "rubbish bin". These aspirations will be treated again as wishful thinking or wishful sinking. Healthy, beautiful, wealthy, happy ships work with dates and calendars. They probably do not get to the destination exactly at the intended time, but getting there a day, or even a month later, is better than not getting there at all.

When you set yourself a goal, set a time and date to achieve it. If you teach your kids to work with goals, do the same for them. If you want to make sure they do not do it stressed and under pressure, let them make their own timetable (and don't call it a deadline, no one is dying here. It is always better to consider it as a celebration date of achievement) and practice estimating how long it will take them to achieve it. You won't believe how this estimation skill can help them in the future.

The crew does not take orders from any other captains (even if it means their parents' captains) but only from the captain of the ship they are on. So, if you hear yourself saying, *"My wife made me"*, *"I didn't do it because of the kids"* or *"Having a family doesn't give me enough time"*, you are excusing yourself from achieving. No one can make you do something without your consent. Your crew did not accept any orders from your wife, kids or family without it going through your captain. On a healthy, beautiful, successful ship, the captain does not use excuses or blame to justify his failures but takes responsibility for his decisions.

Blame and justification for any discomfort or failure is an act of anchor throwing and an inability to lead the ship. It is a sign the person is not feeling in control. If you want to help your children, first be a role model, and never blame them or justify yourself to them. Make sure they know the difference between responsibility and taking blame. It is not the same. Blame is not healthy, even if you blame yourself. Responsibility means you understand that things happened due to choices you have made, and you don't beat yourself up about it but know that next time you will try your best to react differently.

> *Having children makes you no more a parent than having a piano makes you a pianist*
>
> – Michael Levine

Everyone has a parrot on his or her shoulder. Max is there to reflect our thoughts. Max has no filters – he tells us everything we think and believe, whether it is a good thing or not. Max will tell us we are losers if this is what we think, and Max will tell us we are powerful beyond measure if this is what we think. He is a parrot, with no mind of his own. He reflects our fears, our motivation, our desires and he is constantly talking, we constantly listen, even when we think we are not paying attention.

Most of what we think of ourselves we have heard from the people that are closest to us, like our parents and mentors. During childhood, parents have lots of power in making sure their kids' parrot friend, who will escort them for the rest of their lives, will say words of defeat or words of power and encouragement. Some say that Max's accent is very similar to mom or dad's voice. On an easy sail, Max tells us we are capable, healthy, happy, loving, friendly, strong, courageous and wealthy. On a rough sail, Max tells us we are weak, unable, small, helpless, afraid, selfish, gutless and poor. **Successful people control Max by controlling what they think.**

Max will say things he has heard from your family, friends, teachers and other people you have known over the years. He will say things you have heard on TV or read in the paper or will draw conclusions from things that happened in the past. You cannot easily shut him up or blame him for his unstoppable talk. Remember, Max is there all the time and can be very useful to you. When you are all by yourself thinking you may not survive, Max whispers, *"Tomorrow everything will be OK"* (which he probably heard from your dad, in a movie or in a motivational book). **To control what Max says, control what you think.**

It is important to remember that kids are sailing on a separate ship to their parents who drag them with an emotional umbilical cord. When they are young, they do not control much about their surroundings and learn helplessness. There is a window of opportunity during childhood to help your kids by planting thoughts and beliefs that Max will replay whenever they need. Use it wisely! When they become teenagers, their crew will attempt to separate this rope by seeking independence. This is when you cannot keep dragging them and force will not work anymore. On their way to individual sailing, if you try to drag them by force, they will make a choice to sail, far from you.

Max is there, recording everything you say to your kids, to your partner, to your own parents and friends. Imagine he is the voice recorder born with your kids. Max will be with your kids long after you're gone, make sure he will record all the things you would want to say to your kids, when you are not around.

Did you know?

Did you know that 90% of your thoughts, beliefs and actions are controlled by your subconscious? It is also true for your kids.

When trying to motivate your kids, remember that the early years are critical in establishing a very strong, confident "subconscious".

Make conscious decision to plant good thoughts, beliefs and actions in their mind. Their subconscious believes most things Mom and Dad say.

The way we talk to our children becomes their inner voice

– Peggy O'Mara

The war between the two minds

In the war between the conscious and the subconscious mind, the subconscious always wins. Some people say that the mind is like an iceberg. What you see on the surface is just 10% of the size of the iceberg. The subconscious mind hides underneath, controlling most of our behaviors. The older we get, the more conflicts we have between the two. The captain wants to go right, and the crew wants to go left. If the degree of the difference is big, the conflict is big, if the degree of the difference between them is small, the sail will be easy and smooth.

People who are in conflict between the two minds are confused, fearful, upset, angry, disappointed, frustrated and experience various other negative feelings and with this mindset, they lack drive and motivation and they can't really motivate others.

People who establish good relationships between the two minds are happy, focused, successful and appreciative, experience various other happy feelings, and are more driven and motivated and they can easily motivate others. This is exactly the state you want to be in and exactly where you want your kids to be.

 Whatever we plant in our subconscious mind and nourish with repetition and emotion will one day become a reality.

— Earl Nightingale

Summary

✓   We are all sailing the sea of life with captain (conscious) crew (subconscious) and Max (the little voice). The direction we take in life depends on the maps our crew has.

✓   In order to change direction and motivate ourselves or our kids, we must work on the subconscious with focus and clarity and convince our crew that it is safe to do so. Pressure only makes our subconscious resist the change.

✓   If a change lasts 3 days or in best cases a week, it is a sign we did not include our crew in the planning of our journey, and we are de-motivated. Next time, we would need more time to try again.

✓   Each of us has a separate ship and while kids are dragged by their parents' ship with an emotional umbilical cord, their crew is constantly working towards independence. Don't fight it. It is a healthy process. One day they will sail on their own guided by their own captains and crew. You have a window of opportunity during childhood to help them develop safe maps and very supportive parrots.

✓   Do not plant negative orders (fear) in your kids' parrot or try to add it to their map. Picture a positive future so when you are not there, their Max will be your extension in times of trouble whispering, "you can!"

✓   The war between the captain and crew will be there forever. The more we work on the relationship between the two, the easier it will be for us to get what we want.

3 CHAPTER THREE

WHAT IS MOTIVATION?

The first important thing to determine about motivation is the desired outcome. The question you need to ask yourself is:

"Do you want your kids to do something **they** want or something **you** want?"

The reason I am asking this is because the first option is motivating, but the other is not. If you want your kids to do something **you** want, you are trying to manipulate them, and you need manipulation tricks. If you want to encourage your kids to do something **they** want, you are after motivation tricks.

Many parents do not distinguish between the two. They feel that because they have "good intentions" they can mix between them, but manipulation is a formula for disastrous parent-child relationships and encouragement and support are proven formulas for a happy and successful parent- child relationship.

What do your kids want?

If you want to motivate your kids, the first thing you need to do is know what your kids want. By finding what they want, we reveal more of this iceberg and it makes it easier to help them find drive and motivation. The best way to know what they think is to ask. Many parents think they know what their kids want, but never ask. Some say they are too young, some say they do not know what they want, and some are afraid their kids are too influenced by others, but the truth is **your kids' desires are a key ingredient in their success in life**, whether or not they are young, confused or highly influenced.

The task of finding out what your kids think and want is **much easier when they are young**. The reason I believe it is easier in the early years is because their imagination is not limited yet and they allow themselves to want grand things freely and express their desires and dreams.

When kids are young, you can have playing routines at dinner time, driving time, sleeping times, during which everyone gets a chance (and is encouraged) to express themselves.

 The best way to make children good is to make them happy

— Oscar Wilde

Self-expression is a very important skill that kids (and parents too) need in order to be happy and successful. The opposite of self-expression is frustration, frustration, frustration and motivating a frustrated kid is one of the most challenging tasks for parents, being even harder with some age groups. When kids become teenagers after many years of not expressing themselves, it is a lot more challenging to start (but still possible). **If you can, find out what your kids want before they reach frustration.**

Some kids are very comfortable saying what they want. Most kids, however, do not know what they want – they are not sure, they are overwhelmed, and they are more comfortable when prompted to answer questions. I have three kids – 1 boy and 2 girls – and their self-expressions are totally different from each other. There is no need to expect them to have the same level of self-expression, because some of it has to do with their personality and communication style, but **it is possible to encourage all kids, regardless of their personality type, to say what they want.**

"*Success is best measured by how far you've come with the talents you've been given*"

- Anonymous

© *www.ronitbaras.com*

Exercise

In this activity, you, the parent learns to get to know yourself and you help your child get to know him/herself by going through a process of "self-interview". The great thing is that you also get to know each other.

The self-Interview process helps brings to the surface what the crew uses as a guide in the navigating maps. We think many things, but we don't know we think them. When we go through the self-interview and record it, we reveal more of the iceberg and better the relationship between the two.

Did you know?

The first level of emotional intelligence is "recognizing own feelings". Self-interview is a very important stage in developing high emotional intelligence.

If you want children with high emotional intelligence, this is where you start!

Here are the instructions for self-interview and some suggestions for helping your child with his or her self-interview. The questions refer to what your favorite things, qualities, definitions, fears and dreams are and what you think about some things in general. It has many questions that defines who you are at the moment and has the ability to highlight things you have never paid attention to that can motivate you to do and be whatever you want.

Tips for the interview

✓ Print a copy of the list for each of your family members, sit as a family and do it together.

✓ Young kids who cannot read by themselves can do it together with Mom or Dad.

✓ Young kids may find the list too long, so you can do parts of the list over several days or weeks.

✓ Do not be tempted to do it verbally only. Research shows that writing down is more effective in creating focus and being committed to what you think and believe. It is easier later on to refer to a written list than to a verbal statement. Write everything down – it will help you to go over it couple of times before you finalize your thoughts. Writing will allow you to go over it in a year or two and discover how much you have changed. If writing by hand is not for you, use the computer. If recording the interview appeals to you, record it.

✓ Birthdays, New Year's Day, Holidays and special occasion like the first day of school, the last day of term or anything that can be considered a special occasion, are good opportunities to do it.

✓ There are no right and wrong answers – do not look for something that you "should" be thinking. The only thing you should be is yourself!

✓ Some questions have more than one answer – you do not have to stick to one. If there are more, write them all down.

✓ If you work on this list yourself, you are being the best role model.

✓ Ask each other to share and start by sharing yours. Allow people to keep some answers private, but remember which questions anyone asked to keep private and find opportunities to talk about them later one-on-one.

✓ Keep the list somewhere safe with the date and the name of the child. It is awesome memorabilia. Pulling out your kid's list of dreams from age 5 on their 21st birthday can be both amazing and emotional.

✓ Some questions may be hard for young children, for example: what do I think about same sex relationships? Or world hunger? Go over them before to make sure they are **age appropriate**.

✓ Do not use this list to "test" others around you and see if they know you well or test yourself if you know your kids well. It is a formula for trouble.

✓ If anyone participating is stuck on a question, skip and come back to it later. If thinking about it or referring to it later didn't help, asking others what they wrote can help. Sometimes we only need an idea. Only use the asking strategy as a last resort.

My favorites

1. What is my favorite fruit?

2. What is my favorite drink?

3. What is my favorite food?

4. What are my favorite clothes?

5. What is my favorite color?

6. What is my favorite day of the week?

7. What is my favorite movie?

8. What is my favorite song?

9. What is my favorite holiday destination?

10. Who is my favorite singer?

11. Who are my favorite actors?

12. What is my favorite season in the year?

13.   What is my favorite time of the day?

14.   What was my favorite subject at school?

15.   What is my favorite quote?

16.   Who is my favorite friend?

17.   What is my favorite book?

18.   What is my favorite way to pass time?

19.   Who is my favorite family member and why?

20.   What is my favorite game or sport?

21.   What is my favorite birthday gift?

22.   What is my favorite animal?

23.   Who was my favorite teacher of all times?

24.   What is my favorite month? Why?

25.   What is my favorite dream for the future?

My qualities

Knowing what kind of person you are will help you focus your life by improving or avoiding the things you are not good at and doing more of the things you are good at. Motivation and avoidance are triggered by our abilities and mindset. If things are hard, we tend to avoid them, if they are easy and fun, we tend to repeat them with enthusiasm. Lets' explore our qualities.

1.   What do I like about myself?

2.   What do I do well?

3.   What is the skill I would most like to have?

4.   I wish I was better at…

5.   What is the character trait I would never change in myself?

6.   What am I motivated to do?

7.   What am I pessimistic about?

8.   What am I passionate about?

9.   What will help me succeed?

10.   Am I a good friend?

11.   Am I a good child to my parents?

12.   Am I a good parent to my kids?

13.   Am I good with building and maintaining relationships?

14.   What am I proud of?

15.   What am I ashamed of?

16.   What am I frustrated about?

17.   Do I blame or justify a lot?

18.   What makes me angry?

19.   What makes me sad?

20.   What excites me?

21.   What qualities of mine am I happy about?

22.   What qualities will I be happy to get rid of?

23.   What is the worst thing I do to myself?

24.   What am I grateful for?

25.   What do I want to thank my parents for?

My definition of

People define things differently based on the maps their crew uses and what Max whispers in their ears. To find out what is navigating your life, find out your definition to many things in your life. If you think of more questions, add them too.

1.   A good movie is…

2.   A good health is…

3.   Good parenting is…

4.   A good friend is…

5.   Help is…

6.   A good neighbor is…

7.   Being nice is…

8.   Good company is…

9.   A good book is…

10.   A good holiday is…

11.   A good relationship is…

12.   A good marriage is…

13.   A happy lifestyle is…

14.   Financial abundance is...

15.   Good advice is…

16.   Failure is…

17.   It is interesting when…

18.   It is boring when…

19.   It is scary when…

20.   A challenge is…

21.   Life is…

22.   Death is…

23.   Love is…

24.   Jealousy is...

25.   Happiness is…

Did you know?

Research shows that writing down is more effective in creating focus and being committed to what you think and believe. It is easier later on to refer to a written list than to a verbal statement. Do not be tempted to do everything in your head.

My fears

Fears drive our behavior, even when we are not aware of them. Fears of failure, inadequacy or getting hurt make us do "strange" things, lower our confidence and damage our motivation. If you know your fears, you can face them and gradually eliminate them. It may not be easy at first but try to be honest with yourself. It is on your map anyway. I say it is better to know what's blocking you than accepting it as your destiny.

1. What am I afraid of?

2. What makes me angry?

3. Who makes me angry?

4. Who do I blame for my problems?

5. How do I justify my unhappy circumstances?

6. What time of year do I hate most and why?

7. What subject in school did (or still do) I hate most of all and why?

8. What is the scariest time of the day?

9. What is the most uncomfortable situation I have ever experienced?

10. What was the most embarrassing moment of my life?

11. What was the worst day of my life?

12. What was the worst romantic date of my life?

13. What was the worst gift I was ever given?

14. What was the hardest thing I have ever done?

15. What was the worst I have been treated by someone else?

16. When was I discriminated against in my life?

17. What upsets me?

18. What destroys my motivation?

19. What is my worst nightmare?

20. What makes me depressed?

21. What makes me cry?

22. What makes me feel like a failure?

23. What is the worst thing someone has ever told me?

24. When do I feel the loneliest?

25. What was the worst attempt of my life?

My Dreams

What we want and dream of is in the essence of our subconscious and controls much of what we do. Every answer here is valuable and if you ever want to motivate your kids to do something, you need to know what makes them tick. The most important thing is to listen to the answers without judgment or expectations and I promise you will end up with treasures.

1. If I could learn anything I wanted, I would study…

2. If I could go back in time, I would…

3. If I had all the money I wanted, I would…

4. If I could relive one event in life, it would be…

5. If I could erase a moment in life, it would be…

6. If I could meet one person, it would be…

7. If I could wear anything I wanted, I would wear…

8. If I could ask my parents one thing, I would ask…

9. If I could say one thing to my parents, I would say…

10. If I could tell the world one thing, it would be…

11. If I could forget something, it would be…

12. If I could change the world, I would…

13. If I had to spend 1 million dollars in one week, I would spend it on…

14. If I could eat anything I wanted, I would eat…

15.   If I could make someone else love me, it would be…

16.   If I could buy someone I love a gift, it would be…

17.   If I could look like any person I wanted, I would look like…

18.   If I could invent something, it would be…

19.   If I could have 3 wishes, they would be…

20.   If I were an animal, I would be…

21.   If I could visit any place in the world, I would visit…

22.   If I could win the noble prize, it would be for…

23.   If I could make a difference in the world, I would…

24.   If I could be famous, I would be famous for…

25.   If I needed one more chance, I would ask for…

26.   If I could meet the most inspiring person in the world, I would ask to meet…

27.   If I could be in any physical condition, I would…

28.   If I could have a chef cooking all my meals, I would ask the chef to…

29.   If I could choose one birthday party to repeat, it would be…

30.   If I could meet one friend from the past, it would be…

31.   If I could repeat one school year, it would be…

32.   If I could go to my favorite teacher and thank them, it would be…

33.   If there is one thing I am grateful for, it is…

34.   If there is one thing I do not want to lose, it is…

35.   If my house was on fire, the first thing I would save would be…

36.   If I could wake up in the morning knowing how to play a musical instrument, it would be…

37.   If I could write a book, it would be about…

38.   If I had my own plane, I would go to…

39.   If I could buy any gadget, I would buy…

40.   If I could be in any profession I wanted, I would be a…

41.   If I could build any house I wanted, I would make it…

42.   If I could win a big prize, it would be…

43.   If I could win a big prize, I would spend it on…

44.   If I could make someone proud of me, it would be…

45.   If I were a king, I would…

46.   If I were a genie, I would…

47.   If time stood still, I would…

48.   If I could choose one thing that would make me the happiest, it would be…

Know yourself and you will win all battles

– Sun Tzu

Did you know?

Most kids' get their beliefs about themselves and the world around them from the most important people in their life: their parents, family members and educators. They adopt beliefs they are exposed to through observation of verbal and non-verbal communication and do not question their accuracy. The strength of the belief will depend on how close the person is to them, how much they believe this person care about them and how often they are exposed to it. If you want to plant healthy, good, confident and empowering believes in your kids' mind, be close to them, show them you genuinely care about them and repeat the messages you want to instill.

What do I think?

1. What do I think is the most important thing in life?

2. What do I think about school uniform?

3. What do I think about marriage?

4. What do I think about life after death?

5. What do I think about museums?

6. What do I think about TV?

7. What do I think about theme parks?

8. What do I think about war and peace?

9. What do I think is worth dying for?

10. What do I think of family?

11. What do I think is the most valuable object in my life?

12. What do I think about fast food?

13. What do I think about alcohol?

14. What do I think about having pets?

15. What do I think about using animals for medical research?

16. What do I think about celebrities?

17. What do I think about technology?

18. What do I think about global warming?

19. What do you think about using drugs?

20. What do I think about world hunger?

21. What do I think about flying?

22. What do I think about the end of the world?

23. What do I think about science fiction?

24. What do I think about the partner of your dreams?

25. What do I think I will be most famous for?

26.   What do I think we should do to save the world?

27.   What do I think is the most important government department?

28.   What do I think about the role of The United Nations?

29.   What do I think about taxes?

30.   What do I think about love?

31.   What do I think about jealousy?

32.   What do I think about forgiveness?

33.   What do I think should be taught in schools?

34.   What do I think is the best way to run a country?

35.   What do I think about relationships?

36.   What do I think about the importance of friends?

37.   What do I think we should do to people driving under the influence of drugs or alcohol?

38.   What do I think about manners?

39.   What do I think about fairies?

40.   What do I think about love at first sight?

41.   What do I think about humor?

42.   What do I think about using the "F" word?

43.   What do I think about rich people?

44.   What do I think about same-sex relationships?

45.   What do I think about the death penalty?

46.   What do I think about the right amount of sleep people need every day?

47.   What do I think about eating sweets?

48.   What do I think about surprises?

49.   What do I think about black people?

50.   What do I think is the answer to all our problems?

51. What do I think about homeless people?

52. What do I think about domestic violence?

53. What do I think about euthanasia?

54. What do I think we should do with criminals?

55. What do I think about magazines?

56. What do I think about charity?

57. What do I think about volunteering?

58. What do I think about high payments to football players?

59. What do I think about praying?

60. What do I think about sarcasm?

61. What do I think about God?

62. What do I think about learning from history?

63. What do I think about the saying, "All men are created equal"?

64. What do I think about having hobbies?

65. What do I think about diversity?

66. What do I think about abortions?

67. What do I think about relationships with in-laws?

68. What do I think about divorce?

69. What do I think about criticism?

70. What do I think about traveling?

71. What do I think about doctors?

72. What do I think about alternative medicine?

73. What do I think about mediation?

74. What do I think about spirituality?

75.   What do I think about children?

76.   What do I think about teenagers?

77.   What do I think about living in a
      different country?

78.   What do I think about people
      who speak a different language?

79.   What do I think about the battle
      of the sexes?

80.   What do I think about rude
      people?

81.   What do I think about healthy food?

82.   What do I think about liars?

83.   What do I think about camping?

84.   What do I think about performing in front of people?

85.   What do I think is my best quality?

86.   What do I think is important in life?

87.   What do I think about the Christmas holidays?

88.   What do I think about trains?

89.   What do I think about animal cruelty?

90.   What do I think about teamwork?

91.   What do I think about growing old?

92.   What do I think about the impossible?

93.   What do I think is just wrong?

94.   What do I think about art?

95.   What do I think about dressing up?

96.   What do I think about computer games?

97.   What do I think about sales people?

98.   What do I think about gifts?

99.   What do I think about vegetarians?

100.   What do I think about saying "please" and "thank you"?

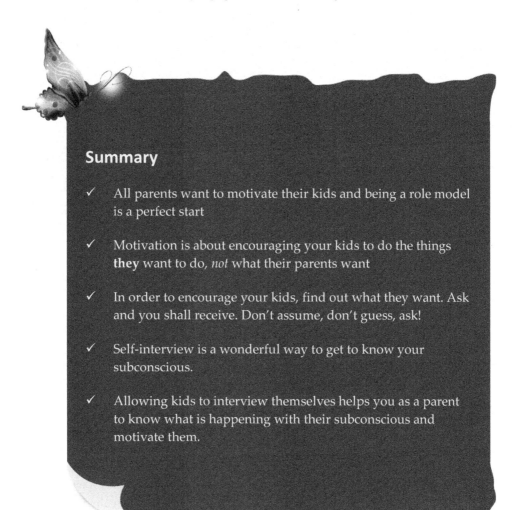

Summary

✓   All parents want to motivate their kids and being a role model is a perfect start

✓   Motivation is about encouraging your kids to do the things **they** want to do, *not* what their parents want

✓   In order to encourage your kids, find out what they want. Ask and you shall receive. Don't assume, don't guess, ask!

✓   Self-interview is a wonderful way to get to know your subconscious.

✓   Allowing kids to interview themselves helps you as a parent to know what is happening with their subconscious and motivate them.

4 CHAPTER FOUR

CHUNKING DOWN

The questions in the previous chapter provide a way to give your kids' "wanting" muscle some good practice and to allow you as a parent to help your kids get what they want in life and be happy. The next step is to chunk each dream down to realistic, day-to-day pieces that do not involve genies, kings, fairies or lottery tickets.

When kids find it hard to get what they want, they go to "fairy land", where magic and fairies (or other grownups) grant them their wishes. Unfortunately, they learn this irresponsible technique from the grown-ups around them. Even parents, when they do not get what they want, go to the "fairy land" of wishing for a winning lottery ticket, drawing a big prize and having more luck, so it is really no wonder their kids do exactly the same. They justify their unhappiness as bad luck or blame someone else for it.

The "fairy land" strategy is not a conscious act but a defense mechanism of our subconscious that supposed to help us manage a "failure" and "disappointment". Imagining a "happy ending" is in fact a good strategy and can really help us but it is a bit limited.

So, I think there is some benefit in developing the imagination with wishes and dreams, but it is very important for kids (and parents) to understand we have the responsibility to create our own luck by actively working towards our goals. If kids want to have friends, they need to do something about it. If kids want to be successful at school, they need to do something about it. If kids want to be able to swim, they need to do something about it. When kids do not wait for things to fall from the sky into their lap and know they have to go actively looking for them, they are empowered. And you as their parents are there to help them succeed.

Exercise

Ask your kids this question:

"If I could help you achieve 3 things in the next 3 months what would they be?"

The "magic 3"

The list of dreams is a good place to start. The task of focusing on three items out of a long list is not easy even for my adult clients. Kids (and grownups) cannot deal with too many things at once and if we ask the crew to change too many things, we are doomed to fail. It is better to choose your battles.

The idea is to get your kids acting and moving towards something they want as quickly as possible and gain success experiences to keep themselves going. Since kids have little practice with goals, we need to make things easy at first. For kids under school age, start with only one goal.

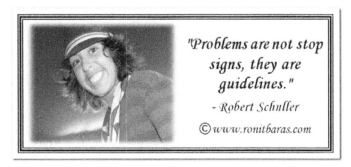

"Problems are not stop signs, they are guidelines."
- Robert Schuller
© www.ronitbaras.com

Most people, even grown-ups are much more successful in reaching their goals if they set them to be achieved within 3 months. This is because it is very hard for the crew to keep focus on one "trip" for longer. They can have longer-term goals and even lifelong goals but then they are called a vision, a purpose but not a goal.

Usually, 3 months is the best kids can manage. Their perception of time is so limited so talking about a life timeframe or even a year timeframe is very challenging for them. Their imagination is a bit limited with this function and they can't see forward that far. This is why it is better to talk to them in "sleeps" – 3 sleeps, 7 sleeps, 30 sleeps and so on. Many times, they are so overwhelmed they can only think one or two weeks ahead. In that sense, the younger they are, the harder it is for them to wait. If your kids are young and restless, help them focus on the next one or two weeks and chunk their goal down so they can achieve something in that short timeframe.

This trick works really well for grown-ups as well. If my clients are a bit more anxious, I ask them to focus on the short term. In severe cases, they only need to focus on the next hour and I ask them, *"What can you do now, sitting next to me, that will make you feel better?"* and the brain searches for the answer straight away. The brain searches and the brain finds.

Tips for using the magic three

✓ Focus on three things you can help them achieve in the next 3 months.

✓ Adjust the question to the right age. Remember the emphasis is on *"helping **you** get what **you** want"*

✓ Make sure your kids ask for something **they** want and not something they believe you want to hear. If you suspect this is the case, ask them *"Why did you choose this?"* or *"What will you get if you do this?"*

✓ Do not belittle any desire or they will keep some desires away from you

✓ Hold yourself back from doing the job for them. Remember you are not the genie. You are just helping them move towards something they want.

✓ Every process of going forward has some setbacks. You want your kids to learn the process. Talk to them about the progress, the movement, the improvement, not about being 100% successful. As long as they are moving forward, they **are** successful

✓ Encourage your kids to write their current goals down somewhere to allow both of you to see them and read them in the next 3 months. If your kids are too young to write, they can draw or cut and paste pictures from a magazine that represents the goal.

- ✓ You can talk about the celebration of the goal as the destination and please be careful about shopping celebrations. When celebrating, the kids need to give themselves the reward, not you and rewards can be small things. It is amazing how many kids want to celebrate achievements with some quality time with parents or friends.

- ✓ Remember to write the date on each of the goal statements, drawings and collages and keep them as memorabilia.

Many kids express being overwhelmed as "too much", "too hard" and even "impossible". Teen kids will have "no chance" thoughts. In this case, chunking down to something you can help them with can make life very easy for them.

Well done is better than well said.

– Benjamin Franklin

The next step of chunking down is using the "magic 3" again. Every problem, every challenge, every desire is chunked down to 3 things.

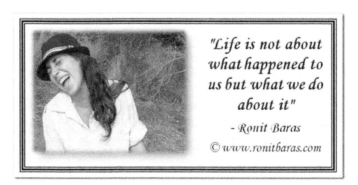

"Life is not about what happened to us but what we do about it"

- Ronit Baras

© www.ronitbaras.com

Did you know?

Writing long-term goals can trigger the "overwhelm" button and promote procrastination as waiting for them increases the sense of failure. The "crew", focusing on more urgent goal, will "file" the goal somewhere in the future and forget about it and thinking of the goal will only remind them they are not achieving it.

Focus on small and short-term goals. Help them accumulate small successes. Research shows that even small achievements can be more motivating then failure.

 **Exercise**

Ask your kids the following question about each one of their top goals:

"To achieve this goal, what are 3 things you can do that will help you get it?"

Notice this question is not about what you can do to make your kid get it but **what they can do** for themselves. When you ask it, you help your kids a lot by facilitating their thinking process. You are transferring the responsibility over the goals to the kids and empowering them.

The reason this question is important is that kids often feel helpless and do not have many ideas and options. In their perception, they are young and do not know enough. Thinking about options is a very good mental exercise and develops the kids' confidence.

Remember it is not your responsibility to come up with ideas. Before you suggest anything, make sure you have given your kids enough time and a "safe space" to come up with their own ideas as this will give them ownership of the solution.

Remember, do not judge or mock any of the ideas your child comes up with. This is the idea of "safe space" –they need to feel safe to think without fear of disappointing you or being ridiculed. If your reaction won't make them feel safe, they will start hiding their thoughts from you, which won't give you what you need, in order to motivate them.

Only if your kid gets too frustrated, teary or angry should you suggest something and even this should be done after you ask, *"Would you like me to suggest something?"* and should be phrased as a question – *"How about ...? Would that be a good idea? What do you think?"*

The reason we ask permission will be discussed in the next chapters of this book and the reason we make it a question is that it leaves a space for kids to consider and not to accept our offer. It is a suggestion. You can take it or leave it and I will still love you and be here to help you. Describing the suggestion as a question leaves the responsibility with the child, which is essential in the art of motivating.

Summary

✓ When kids (and grown-ups) are **overwhelmed, they transfer responsibility** to bad luck and blame others for their problems.

✓ **"Fairy land"** is our outlet to manage failure and disappointment. It is disempowering.

✓ Focus makes perfect. Help your kids start with their **top 3 desires at most**. Use this to help them accumulate success stories.

✓ Start with **short term desires** (3 months maximum) to help kids cope with their limited perception of time. With young kids you can talk about "sleeps" or have a visual calendar to help them wait

✓ Focus on 3 things your kids can **do – action, action, action**! Remember, actions speak louder than words.

✓ Emphasize the process, not the end result

✓ **Suggest only when your kids are feeling lost** and helpless and ask them to approve your offer to suggest and be accepting of their choice (to use your suggestion or not)

5 CHAPTER FIVE

CARROTS AND STICKS

Every person has different motivation drivers. Some people are motivated by "carrots" (encouragement and rewards) and others by "sticks" (threats and punishments). Some want to get something for their efforts and others do things to avoid being hurt or feeling bad. It is all based on our childhood experiences of motivation and our taught definitions of right and wrong.

From the day we are born, everyone around us tells us what is right and what is wrong. Most parents use the "carrot and the stick" to teach kids about right and wrong. Anger and punishment are the stick and smiles and rewards are the carrots. Some parents, following the example of their own parents, even use real sticks, belts and denying of physical touch as punishment, while using physical gestures like a hug and a kiss to say, *"You've made me proud"*.

For school-age children, especially as physical expressions became less and less acceptable, teachers used the form of verbal and written sticks and carrots. If you did the right thing, you got an "A" (I tell my kids it means "Awesome"). If you did the wrong thing, you got an "F". (I don't tell them what that means)

Unfortunately, growing up within "carrot and stick" systems at home, school and work make us form irrational rules of living[1] that say:

"People should always do the right thing. When they behave obnoxiously, unfairly or selfishly, they must be blamed and punished".

---

[1] From Choose to Be Happy by Wayne Froggatt

I have found the best way to give advice to your children is to find out what they want and then advise them to do it

— Harry S. Truman

I guess the difficulty in living with such a rule is assuming there is such a thing as "the right thing" or believing there is a "right way" of doing things, making all other options "wrong". Most parents do use this rule to parent their kids and by that missing out any opportunity to motivate their kids. Think about it this way, if you have to punish your child you have all the proof you need, to know it is not something he wants but something you want so badly you settle for " do it or else" and that is not motivation it is a use of power and a form of bullying.

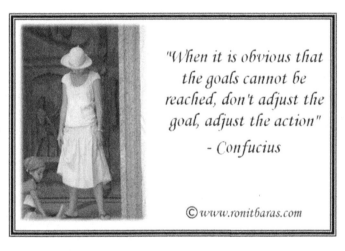

"When it is obvious that the goals cannot be reached, don't adjust the goal, adjust the action"

- Confucius

© www.ronitbaras.com

Whenever I talk to people about right and wrong, I say to them that the difference between right and wrong can only be foretold by those who can read the future.

What is the difference between courage and recklessness?

What is the difference between persistence and stubbornness?

What is the difference between being careful and being a coward?

The difference between them is **the outcome!**

If you climb Mount Everest and come back down alive, you are courageous, but if you fail and die on your way, you are reckless.

If you come up with a working light bulb after 1499 attempts, you are the master of persistence, but until then you are stubborn, and you just do not know when to give up.

If you decide not to buy a house, because you estimate it will drop in value, people call you a careful investor but if house prices go up, people call you a coward.

People can never be sure they are doing the right thing, because they are not fortune-tellers. They estimate everything they do as the best they can do at the time. I do not know anyone who, when making a choice, says, *"Here are my options, I will pick the worst one"*…

"Never, Never, Never give up!"
- Winston Churchill

© www.ronitbaras.com

Carrots are better than sticks

 It is better to bind your children to you by a feeling of respect and by gentleness than by fear

— Terence

Parents who use punishment think it is the way to shift their kids' behavior from doing what is wrong to doing what is right.

Many parents think this is a valid claim and use punishment as a motivator. These parents raise children who also think that punishment and blame are the right way to live.

However, punishment is external and creates fear. It makes people spend their life running away from things they are not happy about, hiding any evidence, stressing about being found out and avoiding action, instead of going towards something they want in life. It is hard to find a crew that will cooperate with this attitude.

Challenges with discipline

Many parents are troubled with making their kids do things. They confuse motivation with discipline.

How to discipline kids? What is discipline and related issues are a source of friction almost in almost every home? Sometimes, the friction is between the two parents. Sometimes, it is between parents and kids and can even be a hot topic in many social gatherings.

The typical definition of discipline 20 or 30 years ago looked like this: mom spends time with the kids, dads work outside the house and power, force and punishments were the way to prepare kids for life when it only taught them fear and obedience.

Discipline is the opposite of motivation and this is certainly true with kids. If you need to discipline your kids, it means you are powerless. It means you are afraid of your kids and that is not good in parenting.

Motivating, encouraging, supporting and helping are acts of **giving**. You do them for the benefit of your kids. Discipline is an act of **taking**. You do it for your own benefit. **As a parent, you need to give, not take.**

Parenting your children is like dancing and you are the one in the lead. It can be a perfect, coordinated dance, in which you move smoothly to the sound of the music, or an awkward dance, like with a lifeless puppet.

Yes, you can use force and your kids will dance along, but they will be lifeless. They will hate you, disrespect you, and when they have a hard time, they will not come to you for support and will never ask for your help,

How many parents do you know that say to their kids who have done horrible things, *"Why didn't you come to me for help?"* They used force and abused their parental powers to make their children do what the parents wanted and then they complain that the kids do not come and ask for help? Where is the surprise?

When your kids do not come to ask you for help, this is when you have lost the opportunity to help them grow and make sure their Max will be there to help them in time of trouble. You are failing to protect them.

I strongly recommend that every parent abandon the desire to discipline. If you think in terms of discipline, you have already lost your power and your credibility with your kids. Many parents think that disciplining the kids is part of the "job description" and this is what makes parenting seem so hard.

I personally know many parents who have many problems with their kids and search for schools that will discipline them. They say, *"I have problems with my kids, and I need a school that can discipline them"*, but they do not understand that it is a vicious cycle. Parents searching for power, send their kids to schools that search for power and no matter how you look at it, the kids come out of the other side, powerless.

If you give up discipline, you will not have problems and you will not need a school to discipline your kids. I encourage you to stay away from this way of thinking. From my experience, it is the way to lose your kids at an early stage. In many houses, there are conflicts between parents about the "right way to discipline" which I consider an oxymoron.

Right and discipline cannot go hand in hand. Discipline is taking and it is never right for parents to argue about the right way to "take" from their own kids.

Conflict between parents over discipline, contributes greatly to the kids' behavior. If this is your case, I suggest you spend time with your partner and discuss your differences around parenting, encouragement, discipline, authority and the best way to raise good kids instead of talking about the best way to discipline kids.

Otherwise, your kids may take advantage of this conflict while suffering emotionally. It is best to do it when you are both happy and relaxed, when the kids are not around and there is no problem you need to sort out. When people are happy, they can think better. It is best for a couple to discuss such topics even before they bring kids to the world, but it is never too late to align philosophies and attitude.

I know that many parents debate this topic a lot. I have lived around the world and have been involved with so many communities and I know firsthand that having doubts about your parenting is worse than making mistakes. Parents are not perfect and that is what makes us human.

The core skills we need in parenting are love and the desire to improve. I think these are the core skills in life. Love can do a lot more than discipline. I know it sounds like a cliché, but the desire for power does not go hand in hand with love.

 Where did we ever get the crazy idea that in order to make children do better, first we have to make them feel worse? Think of the last time you felt humiliated or treated unfairly. Did you feel like cooperating or doing better?

– Jane Nelson

Did you know?

Children will not judge their parents for actions their parents believed in but rather judge them for being inconsistent or behave in a way that was incongruent with their own beliefs and values.

Focus on developing a parenting philosophy that is consistent and mindful. Do not use parenting strategies just because they are the strategies you know. Question them!

If you adopt the mindful parenting style, you will be consistent and project confidence. Even if your kids will not use the same strategy with their own kids, they will appreciate you for being mindful and consistent.

 Exercise

When you experience a small panic attack when your kids do not meet your expectations, ask yourself these questions:

"Why do I expect them to do this differently?

Did my parents think the same about me?

Did I like the way my parents expressed their expectations?

What are the risks of following what my parents did?

Do I agree with my partner about those expectations?

If my child behaves like this, what does it mean to me?

If my child behaves like this, does it mean they will be like this when they grow up?

Am I strong enough to support my child or do I seek power because I feel weak?"

Remember, kids can do anything you present in an encouraging way. They will be confident and strong if you help them move forward with small, gentle pushes, but if you push too hard, they will fall and then resist.

Think of your kids as they took their first steps. You never pushed them to walk. You stretched your arms wide open and around them to protect them from falling and you moved back so they could come towards you. It is the same with every new thing they do, even behavior. Small pushes towards a place they want to go is encouragement. Big pushes against where they want to go or worse, where you want them to go, are a form of violence.

You probably want to give your children many values. Do not focus on discipline so they do not think this was your gift to them. The only people who can fire parents are their kids and they can only do it when they have their own kids and they understand what parenting means. I will know I am fired, big time, if my grownup kids ever say, *"My mom was a good mother, because she knew how to discipline me"*. This will be the sign that I have sentenced them to be in the approval trap all their life. (More on the approval trap in the next chapter)

> Rewards and punishments are the lowest form of education
>
> – Chang Tzu

I would like to encourage you to shift away from sticks and towards carrots. In my opinion, sticks are short-term motivators, but they are draining and stressing both for parents and for kids and the crew reacts badly to their presences. Success on a test to avoid negative parental reaction has an expensive emotional price attached to it – fear, stress and loss of trust. I promise to give you many tools in this book to be able to make this shift in an easy and smooth way. You just have to use them.

Tips for parenting without discipline

✓ When your kids do things you perceive as wrong, do not punish them because this will draw attention to the behavior you do not want.

✓ Find the opposite desirable behavior and when they do it, reward them for it. Instead of saying, "You should not play with your food", wait for them to eat the way you expect them to and say, "It is wonderful to see you're eating so nicely". Whenever you are upset about your kids' behavior, remember that carrots are better than sticks.

✓ Imagine that each person is a ship. Each time the person accepts blame for something, it is like throwing an anchor overboard – it slows them down and makes it harder for them to keep going, and if they throw too many of them, they will get stuck.

✓ Teach your kids to take responsibility. Give them choices. Make sure they understand they may not always control what happens to them, but they can always control how they react to it.

✓ Change your perception about obnoxious behavior, because it is always a cry for help.

✓ Listen carefully when kids behave like this and lend them a hand. Punishing a child who behaves obnoxiously is like hitting them for having the courage to ask for help. Instead, offer them words to describe their feelings.

✓ Change your perception about fairness and selfishness. The world is not fair, there is no global fairness committee and you are not the president of this committee. People always do what they think is good for them and they cannot take care of their interests at the same time as taking care of the entire world's interests.

✓ Teach your kids that they are the most important people in their world, and they should never ever compromise their interests to gain anyone else's love, affection or approval. Not even yours. Yes, I know, it might make it a bit harder to parent them, but they are going to communicate with thousands of people throughout their lives and many more years than being at home, so give up this illusion of control for their own sake.

Summary

✓ Everything we do is motivated by either **sticks and carrots**

✓ **Carrots are better than sticks**. Using sticks is a form of punishment and carrots' taste last longer and can help us in times of trouble.

✓ **Using sticks too often** will make your child avoid asking for help and you miss out on the opportunity to positively influence what Max, the parrot will say, when you are not there.

✓ **Do not confuse motivation and discipline**. Motivation is for the child's sake. Discipline is for the parents' sake.

✓ Motivation is a form of giving and discipline is a form of taking. Powerful parents give. Weak parents take.

✓ **Do not confuse personal strength and power**. When you are strong, confident and respectful, you are powerful but never have to use it.

✓ When kids do not follow your expectations, go through the **reflection process** to assess what it really means instead of reacting automatically.

✓ **Conflicts between parents** on forms of discipline/motivation, contribute badly to kids' behavior.

✓ **Small, gentle pushes** can make kids walk a long way and work way better than pushing them.

6 CHAPTER SIX

THE APPROVAL TRAP

I am fortunate to live in tropical Queensland, Australia, have a beautiful deck facing my big garden, with ferns, palm trees, and coach all my clients facing this beauty throughout our sessions. I would like to share with you a story of one of my clients who was trapped big time in the approval trap and use this for you as a warning. **Trapped parents cannot motivate. Trapped kids cannot be motivated.**

The desire to get approval is the biggest block in self-motivation and in motivating others. If you want to be able to motivate your kids, you need to make sure neither you nor your kids seek approval as this goes against the subconscious' guidelines.

It was a lovely day on my life coaching deck and Talia came over wearing her gorgeous bright-colored dress, but it did not help lighten up her spirit. She was very sad. I had known her for a while and admired her deeply. Talia was an example of perfection for me. She was beautiful, she was friendly, she was knowledgeable, she was in a relationship, she had a perfect job and she was amazingly smart. She played musical instruments (yes, more than one), sang and already held several degrees. While other people struggled to manage their time, she had worked full time and completed three degrees with high scores. She had travelled the world volunteered to help women in need. And she had done all that by the age of 25.

Still, Talia was a very sad and tormented woman, because nothing she did seemed to please her mother.

Talia was in what I call the approval trap.

Unfortunately, we are all born into that trap without a choice. The way things are structured when we are young is that we seek our parents' approval to learn about life and build our confidence. Living every day of our life around them makes them almighty gods for us and we do everything within our tiny power to get their approval.

It is amazing how many grownups looking for emotional relief are in fact in the approval trap, as if they are caged inside that childhood belief that their existence depends on what their parents think of them.

At the beginning, it starts as a way for us to define who we are and forms an integral part of our socialization process. Our parents give us their approval of things they consider right and disapproval of things they consider wrong. Eating with your fingers at the age of two is cute. At the age of three, it is met with *"Not with your hands, sweetie. Here, take this spoon"*. When you are 5 years old and you play with your food, it brings on loud disapproval from your parents.

Our parents' approval may not be essential to our existence, but it quickly becomes essential to our emotional survival.

However, instead of using approval as a socializing tool and a way to teach independent thinking, some parents use approval as a way to control their kids. Those kids, like Talia, grow living their life in a continuous, fruitless, endless pursuit of their parents' approval.

In the movie "Despicable Me", Gru shows his mother his various inventions as he grows up and she just shrugs her shoulders and says "eh", even at the sight of a masterpiece. Watching that, I said to myself, *"This is probably how kids in the approval trap end up living – in a constant attempt to show their parents their masterpieces and be in constant disappointment"*.

Talia had already produced thousands of masterpieces. Her life was so dedicated to creating masterpieces that would finally win her some approval that it had exhausted her completely.

The report card approval trap

Around the age of 5 or 6 (depending on where they are in the world), children are introduced to more people who give (or deny) them their approval – their teachers. School is a place that teaches kids how to seek approval from Day One. You need permission to move, to sit, to stand, to go to the toilet, talk to someone else and almost everything is dictated for you, including the clothes you wear and the kids you spend time with.

After a short time at school, you can tell that those socializing agents use approval and disapproval to control you and if you do not get it quickly enough, they make it painfully obvious with punishments.

To illustrate just how quickly kids are forced into submission, let me tell you about something that happened to me 30 years ago, when I was running the Creative Thinking Project in Grade 1 with 6-year-olds.

It was the second half of the year and I was going to teach the kids geometry, fractions and math in a very intuitive and fun way using double mirrors. I gave each child a piece of paper and asked them to scribble on it. I told them that the more they scribbled on the page, the more fun they would have and the more beautiful the double mirrors will make it look. More scribbling would also make it easier for them to understand the concepts of multiplication, geometry and fraction. What I did not take into consideration was that we would have an issue with … scribbling.

The kids looked at me in shock and asked, *"What do you mean?"* I took a piece of paper and scribbled on it. *"Look"*, I said, *"Just like this. It's really simple"*, but the kids were even more shocked. Reluctantly, they started drawing on their sheets of paper houses, flowers and clouds and then scribbled over them. It took me a while to figure out that scribbling was the "wrong" way of drawing. They thought I wanted them to ruin their own drawings and did not see the point.

These kids were so young, yet they were already programmed to think that scribbling was inappropriate. When they were younger and drew whatever they could, their socializing agents must have said things like, *"That's not drawing. That's just scribbling"*. Eventually, they just stopped trying.

I kept encouraging them to scribble more and more and when they finished, I told them to sign their names on their colorful creations, *"Like real artists"*. They were convinced I was totally nuts.

Instead of teaching free thinking and creativity at school, they teach obedience. Schools manage to convince kids (and their parents) that report cards are written certificates of your worth through your teachers' approval (in fact, report cards are equally there to measure how good the teachers are, but they would rather parents and kids didn't know that or considered that to be the case). Signs of individuality are not approved and, in some places, the "tall poppy syndrome" (keep your head down and be like everybody else) is nearly an official school policy.

Unfortunately, even university does not teach free and creative thinking but mostly conformance and narrow-mindedness. When our daughter Eden was 24 years old, she studied at one of the best psychology departments in the world, and many of her teachers read their PowerPoint presentations word for word. You get bites of information, chew on them before exams and then spit them out again on the exam sheet and the better you do it, the sweeter the taste of approval is.

Did you know?

Research on successful people discovered that that many of them were not particularly successful in school, did not perform academically, dropped out of school or were "different" in some way. The surprising results of the research were that most of them were highly supported by their parents for being "different".

If your child is not a "mainstream" child, remember that supportive parents make the difference between success and feeling bad about being different.

Ticket to Heaven

The approval trap appears in many aspects of our life. While spirituality gives people a sense of purpose, direction, serenity and happiness, organized religion gives some individuals a sense of control over others instead. If you follow the rules, you are approved and get a ticket to Heaven. Some people even believe they can get on a fast track to Heaven by convincing others to follow their rules (like multi-level marketing, where you get more rewards if you find someone who will find someone who will find someone who will buy … or not, because by that stage, who cares? You have gained your ticket already).

Do not get me wrong. I am not against convincing others. I am a teacher, convincing kids that they are wonderful, amazing, talented, friendly and courageous is a main part of my job description. In coaching, I do the same as the network marketers. I try to create a ripple of happiness.

I believe that my purpose is to help people find happiness and I hope their happiness will help others find happiness and hopefully the cycle will never end (maybe it will entitle me to a ticket to Heaven on Earth). I believe in convincing but not in "my way is the highway". There are many ways to happiness, and I encourage everyone to find their own ways rather than using Ronit's product.

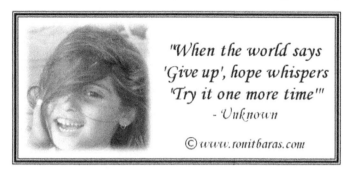

"When the world says 'Give up', hope whispers 'Try it one more time'"
- Unknown

© www.ronitbaras.com

I am very concerned about how many "seek approval" messages my kids are exposed to today. The songs they hear are full of *"I am nothing without you"* (my kids love Bruno Mars). The TV is full of *"I must have this to be cool"* messages and movies are "full of horrible attention-seeking heroes, like Megamind and Despicable Me (and even Up), and I am helpless against them. I am sure there were similar songs when I was younger. I just did not have the critical thinking then to judge them. Even now, I catch myself singing a song with the kids in the car and suddenly, I notice the lyrics and discover that yet again, the singer is helpless and needs someone else to make him/her fulfilled, happy or alive.

"People often say that motivation doesn't last. Neither does bathing - that's why we recommend it daily"
- Zig Ziglar

© www.ronitbaras.com

What others think about you

I was born into the approval trap. My family members, much like everyone else around us, were very busy directing their lives according to what others thought about them. I was very lucky to wake up at the age of 16 and realize that by seeking approval I was compromising everything that was dear to me.

You see, my mom and dad grew up in the approval trap and passed it on to me. Until the age of 16, I thought that navigating life based on what others thought about me or my actions was the only way to think. Until then, I never questioned why we were getting dressed, why we went to school or why my parents had to go to work. In our house, the only answer was *"So other people won't say <insert*

something negative here> about us". Only much later, I discovered this was **negative focus** – instead of doing something for yourself, you do it to avoid something worse, something more painful. This kind of a trap brings you to a state of avoidance. Instead of trying new things, you beat yourself up for thinking or doing something that just might attract negative thoughts from others.

While Talia was only trapped by the need for her mom's approval, those who function according to what "others" think about them are in a worse position. You see, Talia's mom was very consistent, so Talia had to fit into her mom's standards, but what do you do when you need to fit into many other people's standards?

You live for others!

You compromise what is important to you all the time!

You are in constant fear!

You develop a sense of inadequacy!

It is very important to understand that we are social creatures and our desire to have a sense of belonging makes us dependent on some form of "approval" from our society. What we call "socialization" – the process of learning what is acceptable in our society and what is not – involves kids' main "socializing agents" – their parents, their teachers and other family members – giving them messages of approval and disapproval. So, unless we live all by ourselves, totally isolated and without any human contact, we can never claim that we do not need approval at all.

We define our identity through our communication with the people around us. We experience things and get feedback that directs us towards a desired, productive and agreeable behavior. Even the words we use require some form of *agreement*. For example, if I started writing here in another language, you would leave the page and even get a bit angry at me, because we do not have an agreement that I can write to you in a different language.

It is not easy to recognize when external approval becomes a kind of social trap. In fact, many people reject the idea by saying that we cannot really live without approval, which is true. Many social norms bring a lot of stability to a group of people living together, but it is good to question them from time to time.

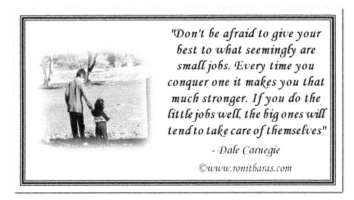

"Don't be afraid to give your best to what seemingly are small jobs. Every time you conquer one it makes you that much stronger. If you do the little jobs well, the big ones will tend to take care of themselves"

- Dale Carnegie

©www.ronitbaras.com

The fact that we sometimes consider encouragement to be approval is not a real problem. There is no person on Earth that does not enjoy it and feel good about it. The problem arises when we are sucked into an approval power game, because it is addictive and turns approval into a need for us.

Wanting to be loved, accepted, part of a group, approved or a source of pride for someone, are all-natural feelings that help us succeed in life, but when we cannot succeed (or function) without them, we are trapped. It happens slowly, like putting a frog in hot water and heating the water slowly, so the frog cannot feel it is being cooked slowly up to its death.

When people are young, they watch their families in this trap and think to themselves, "That's life. Therefore, I must do the best I can for others to love me, accept me and approve of all my actions, thoughts and ideas"[2].

When they become teenagers, a conflict starts between finding significance and getting love and connection and it is very painful. With every action, teenagers ask themselves, "How much of my uniqueness should I sacrifice for others to love me?" (my book Be Special, Be Yourself for Teenagers is dedicated to this dilemma).

Those who find the balance between the two and understand that we cannot live completely on our own and must compromise slightly, succeed. Those who compromise

---

[2] From Choose to Be Happy by Wayne Froggatt

most of the time or compromise on everything have officially fallen into the approval trap.

Unfortunately, most teenagers are in that trap already. If you examine their home environment, you will find that most of them live with parents who are also trapped.

By adulthood, most people are already in that trap. They are mature enough to be independent by law, but they are dependent in their thinking. As adults, we adopt concepts of status, fashion and coolness. Some of us do everything to stick out, make people think highly of us and feel significance and approval. Some of us do everything to blend in and feel accepted.

Either way, we remind ourselves just how low our self-esteem is and develop a dependence on others. This causes stress and anxiety in our lives as we compromise our health, happiness and wellbeing for external standards. We then have relationships based on mutual approval (and break them up when there is not enough approval anymore), we bring kids into the world and the cycle starts again.

Most people, in fact, 90% of them, do not have an answer to *"Why do you do what you do?"* If they do answer, it is with another question they cannot answer *"Isn't it what I'm supposed to do"* or *"Isn't it what everyone else is doing?"*

No!

"Supposed to" and "everyone else" are part of the trap. When you make others more important in your decision-making, in your mind, you do not have much say in any matter in your life. The crew does not like this at all.

There you have it, a formula for disaster.

Because one believes in oneself, one doesn't try to convince others. Because one is content with oneself, one doesn't need others' approval. Because one accepts oneself, the whole world accepts him or her.

— Lao Tzu

Drugs and drug dealers

 When everyone zigs, zag!

— Marty Neumeier

People often like "zigging" (being like everyone else), because of their high need for certainty. They think that going with the crowd reduces their risk and, in some ways, it does.

When my husband, Gal and I lived in Thailand, we had a rule of eating where there were lots of people already. Yes, we needed to wait a bit longer for our food, but it was usually a sign that the food was fresher and tastier. Many people already eating the same food reduced our risk, so zigging can be very useful.

However, there are some parts of life where following the herd is taking away your control, like when you take drugs because your friends do. You see, the approval trap is like an addiction. It starts nicely and with lots of pleasure, but the more you use it, the more you need it and the more of it you need. Pretty soon, you cannot go back to the times when you made your own decisions and choose whether to live by others' rules or not. You are hooked and you walk around like a junky, looking for your next approval "shot".

Parents who raise kids into the approval trap are like drug dealers. They provide their kids with the drug and use it to control their kids. I know it is hard to consider it that way, but most parents are drug dealers, dealing with approval as a way to gain power. Those parents gain an imaginary power for a short time, when their kids are their custody, but they sentence their kids to be "users" for the rest of their life.

The first step in getting out of this trap is admitting you are the drug dealer. It is tough, I have to admit, but please bear in mind that if you are trapped, you are there because you are in a cycle that you have never chosen to create. If you are a "drug" dealer, it is not your fault. The only fault is not stopping the cycle. It was never your choice to use approval as a parenting tool, but you do have the choice to break the cycle. You are doing it for your kids' sake. Trapped parents raise trapped kids.

Here is a simple way to find out if you are suffering from Approval Addiction. The formula to painful life is "When you take something that makes you feel good and it turns into a need, you lose control of your feelings and you give your feelings control over you". When you make the desire for approval a need that you cannot live without and direct your life around it, you sentence yourself to life in prison. It is a special prison, because you are the prisoner and the prison guard – it is all in your head.

 Exercise

If you want to make sure you are not your kids' "drug dealer", make sure you are not addicted to approval yourself. The first step is recognizing that you are caged by a mindset that blocks you from being happy and fulfilled – that you are the one giving others power over your life.

To find out if you are trapped, answer the following questions:

1. **In my own family, which parent wanted me to obey him/her?**
   A parent seeking obedience is usually a parent who confuses parenting and discipline. This parent is weak or lack skills to do things differently. Again, you want to assess your own traps and not be judgmental. Try to be forgiving. If someone grows in a house with a parent or parents who are "drug dealers", you can't blame him/her for considering this a parenting style and doing the same thing with their own kids.

2. **Which parent do I mostly want to impress? Why? How do I do that?**
   Many times, we want to impress the one that does not give us approval or use his/ her approval to manipulate us. Remember, they do not have to approve of what we do but they have to approve of us, with our faults and mistakes. I am not happy with everything my son does, but I accept the fact he does the best he can with the skills, abilities, fears and mindset he has. None of his actions is done against me. He probably does things because somehow, he thought he would benefit from them.

3. **Was this parent in the approval trap him/herself?**
   If so, be loving and accepting. It only means he/she was not able to stop the cycle, but you can.

4. **Who are the people in my life I care the most about** what they think of me? In this list, you can find your own "drug dealers"?

5. **What are the good things people say about me** that make me happy? How do I feel if they don't say it? Or if they say the opposite (this will help you find the substance they use to control you)?

6. **How do you I feel when I hear someone complimenting others?**

7. **What make me feel special/ significant?**

8. **Who do I expect to make me feel special/ significant?**

9. **What do I do to make myself feel special/ significant?**

10. **How do I feel when people don't ask me to give them service that is my profession?**

People in the approval trap have some common character traits; all related to fear (is there anything besides love and fear?). They lack significance, have low self-esteem and use attention-seeking behavior to gain more significance, although that cannot remove the fear or raise their self-esteem.

Trapped individuals have the idea that to be highly thought of by some important others, they need to stick out, gain superiority by making others feel inferior, pretend to be someone they are not or, in other cases, never take risks to avoid conflict and judgment.

Did you know?

Most therapies revolve around the "approval trap". The therapist will search for the source of the trap and help the client question the validity of the belief regarding self-worth and self-acceptance. If you want to keep your kids away from therapists, do not use approval as a parenting strategy.

Exercise

Everyone is trapped somehow, but what matters is how deeply. Use the list of approval-seeking behaviors below to discover if you are trapped or not and how deep are you in the trap of approval.

Give each item a rating from 0 to 10 (0 means you never do it and 10 means you do it all the time). My suggestion is to focus on those you gave high scores, indicating you have that behavior and at the end of this chapter, I will give great tips to change that and get yourself out of the trap.

1.   Immediately approving things others say

2.   Agreeing with others just to avoid a conflict

3.   Changing your mind easily with little pressure

4.   Changing your statements based on the audience

5.   Looking for ways to be seen by others – trying to be the center of the attention in parties, meetings and family gatherings

6.   Seeking recognition (awards, prizes, being the best)

7.   Never returning a faulty product (to avoid conflict)

8.   Being very fashion conscious

9.   Needing company to succeed

10.   Ending sentences with a question seeking approval (*"It looks good, doesn't it?"*) or using a question tone for statements

11.   Being devastated by low scores on exams or bad reviews

12.   Blaming others for your feelings ("How can I be happy when she doesn't like me?")

13.   Pushing your kids to have high academic achievements (as a symbol of status)

14.   Having a bad relationship with your parents (every sad relationship with parents originates from disapproval. One of them did not approve of the other and this was the source of the conflict)

15. Buying brand names

16. Being scared to be alone

17. Attention seeking behavior (for kids it is making noise or being a troublemaker. For grownups, it is doing the opposite of what the majority does or doing things excessively)

18. Being subject to peer pressure

19. Being very particular with your words to sound smart and knowledgeable

20. Hesitating to share your opinion

21. Compromising to gain popularity

22. Being overly polite

23. Being afraid to say "No" to someone asking you for something you do not want to give (like your time)

24. Punishing your kids if someone complains about them but never asking the kids what really happened (kids are not a threat, but others are)

25. Continually asking others to tell you what they think about you, your clothes, your new furniture, etc.

26. Drinking alcohol because your friends do

27. Being jealous of the success of others (as if their success takes some of the attention away from you)

28. Accepting invitations to events you do not want to attend

29. Having a fear of authority (perceiving authority as power rather than inspiration or guidance)

30. Telling others that you hold a secret you will not share to make yourself feel special (*"I know something you don't"*)

31. Being a follower rather than a leader

32. Pointing out people's mistakes (to look good compared to them)

33. Thinking of yourself as "not good enough" ("enough" for who/what?)

34. Flattering someone to get their approval (teachers' pet)

35.   Not standing up for your rights

36.   Telling others you know something they do not and saying you can teach them that thing

37.   Blaming others for your life's circumstances

38.   Calling other names to make them feel inferior and then feel better by comparison *("this stupid person", "that was so dumb")*

39.   Being obsessively jealous of a partner (wanting to be the only person they are in contact with)

40.   Lending money although you do not want to

41.   Being preoccupied with symbols of status

42.   Playing "one up" (anything you can do, I can do better)

43.   Continually searching for signs of appreciation

44.   Being afraid of doing funny things (to avoid being perceived as ridiculous)

45.   Not doing cute, innocent things for fear of being perceived as childish

46.   Playing Devil's Advocate in discussions (must stick out somehow)

47.   Seeking compliments from others

48.   Humiliating others when they ask for a favor or help (low self-esteem and aiming to feel important)

49.   Being afraid to tell about good things that happen to you in fear the others might say you are bragging

50.   Helping your friends move when you have something else to do

51.   Having special dishes for guests

52.   Not inviting guests home for fear of what they might say later about you and how you live

53. Initiating conflicts and having constant arguments (using arguments to scare others and make them feel inferior for a false belief that this makes you superior)

54. Feeling humiliated with low income (what will others say about me?)

55. Smoking or taking drugs because others do

56. Taking control over conversations (wanting others to think highly of you and using every opportunity to impress)

57. Feeling humiliated around educated people for not having more education

58. Exaggerating when telling stories about yourself (to be perceived as more successful, more capable or richer)

59. Staying in contact with people you do not like because you "have to" (parents, siblings, friends)

60. Being competitive

61. Witnessing injustice but never saying anything about it

62. Manipulating people to give you what you want (thinking that getting what you want is approval)

63. Looking for instant gratification and finding it hard to wait for things to happen your way (*"If things do not happen the way I want, it may be a sign of disapproval"*)

64. Having millions of excuses to make yourself look better

65. Having to present your opinion on every occasion

66. Coming late to every event (attention seeking)

67. Cleaning the house in panic before guests come

68. Apologizing too much

69. When talking to others, using statements like *"you must do this"* or *"you have to tell him"* to boost your own confidence

70. Worrying when someone disagrees with you (not being able to accept disagreements)

71. Giving your spiritual leader the power to make decisions for you

72. Being overly busy with other people's ulterior motives (*"I have to know what she really thinks"*)

73. Feeling shame

74. Being shy – shyness is sometimes a result of fear of saying the wrong thing

75. Feeling insulted or humiliated when people express an opinion that is an opposite to yours

76. Being a drama queen (or king)

77. Being a rescuer or a savior (to be liked by others)

78. Being aggressive (using aggressiveness to hide low self-esteem and scare others)

79. Feeling self-pity – feeling sorry for yourself and saying it out loud (attention seeking)

80. Hesitating to talk in front of others (did you know most people are more afraid of public speaking than death?)

81. Pretending to be very busy when invited to events/gathering (so many people want me to come and I need to choose between them)

82. Being anxious to know what others think about you

83. Putting others down (thinking their bad position will give you an advantage)

84. Being judgmental towards others (again, presenting others as inadequate or with bad judgment implies that you are in a better position)

85. Having the fear of failure

86. Being indecisive (looking for the perfect decision that will make you look best)

87. Constantly asking permission from someone to do things (a sign of fear)

88. Trying to control others (for fear of the others doing things differently)

89. Saying others are *"full of themselves"* to make them look bad next to you

90. Continually telling others what you expect from them (to feel strong, powerful and significant)

91. Following the majority when making decisions (thinking that if most people do it, it is probably the right thing to do)

92. Obsessively checking yourself over and over again before submitting something (proposal, test, assignment, report or article)

93. Lying – every form of lying is done for approval. People lie to make themselves look good, because they think the truth will not be to their favor

94. Feeling guilty

95. Strictly clinging to tradition (safe and pre-approved!)

96. Being angry with your family member or friend for choosing to move away and live in another place (their choice being an indication they do not agree with your choice to stay, which may have nothing to do with reality)

97. Telling stories about bad things that are happening to you (must stick out somehow)

98. Gossiping about others (to make them look bad in comparison or win social favor)

99. Pretending to know something you do not (so others think highly of you)

100. Bragging about yourself (the other side of seeking significance and attention)

Find out the behaviors you have and start working on the ones with the highest ratings.

If you have completed this activity, you probably understand that it is impossible to be totally free from needing approval. Again, do not blame yourself or others for this mindset, because you always do the best you can, and your parents always did the best they could. But now that you know how dangerous approval can be to live with, you cannot afford to pass it on to your children, because doing what was done to you is no longer the best you can do. When you search for a motivation tool, it is important to understand that **approval can motivate but disapproval does the opposite**. To change, we need to make a conscious decision to change!

If you need some help in motivating yourself to change, think of how much pain you have endured over the years while seeking others' approval and about how much more heartache and pain you will have to endure in a year, 5 years and 10 years if you do nothing.

Think how cruel you will be to your kids by continuing this cycle. My mentor life coach did this trick to me when I faced a difficult change. He said to me, *"Would you want your daughter to be like this?"* and I understood that I managed to live with the pain as a survival mechanism, but I could not live with the pain of being a role model to my daughter and making her suffer for it. I made the change immediately!

The good news is that you can minimize several approval-seeking behaviors at once by developing a single skill. For example, if many of your approval-seeking behaviors are due to lack of significance, working on your sense of uniqueness and learning to feel special will reduce or even eliminate about a third of the behaviors mentioned.

Obviously, each solution requires time and energy, and reading it is not going to make the change, but implementing it and making a habit of it will. My suggestion is to pick one skill a week and to do something that will help you develop that skill every day. This way, over 21 days (it takes 21 days to create a habit) you can slowly develop your self-confidence and get yourself out of that trap. Once you are out of this trap, motivating your kids to be independent thinkers will be easy.

People like Talia who are actively working towards getting out of that trap, express feelings of freedom, control and happiness. You can feel the same! By default, your kids will feel the same.

I tell all my clients that when we make a change, we need the help our subconscious mind, which quietly works in the background to protect us. During years of living by other people's rules, the subconscious is convinced we are a risk to ourselves and we are not capable of taking control of our lives. If you feel that you are out of control and you have thoughts of giving other people the power over your life, it is because your subconscious is now protecting you … from yourself!

Those tips done consciously will go a long way to convince your subconscious that you are a wonderful, capable and independent person and your behavior will gradually change, as if by magic.

You can also use them to develop those skills in your kids, so they can send early messages to their "crew" that they are in control, wonderful, capable and independent.

Tips for getting out of the approval trap

✓ Develop Critical thinking – sit every day and actively question everything around you. For a whole week, question your tradition, your belief system, the reason you go to work, your lifestyle, your parents' style of parenting, your own parenting style and so on.

✓ Develop a responsible attitude – remember that no one can make you feel anything and no one else is responsible for your feelings or actions. When talking to people, instead of using phrases like, "You make me angry/sad/disappointed", say, "I feel angry/sad/disappointed". Instead of explaining, "I don't have money", say, "I've made a choice not to use the money for this". This will send your subconscious a message that you are taking control.

✓ Practice independent thinking with help – sit down with yourself, a very good friend or a life coach, when others are not there and examine your thoughts without pressure. Ask yourself, "What do I really think about working late hours?" and be honest with yourself. You may not say it to others immediately, but at least you will not confuse what others want you to think with what you think yourself.

✓ Associate with the right crowd – people in the approval trap cannot afford to associate with other people who are trapped, because they reinforce the existing beliefs and behaviors. Find people who stick out for being confident, who do not show all the behaviors on the list, and spend time with them. They will not try to impress you and you will not have to try to impress them.

✓ Develop a sense of uniqueness – make a list of things you are good at and find things to master. They do not have to be academic. They can be any skill, like good time management, being a great cook, being expert at your job and even being a good parent. We all have skills. The more you know it, the less you need others to tell you.

✓ Build your self-esteem – yes, I know, this one is a big ask and one week will not be enough. It is more of a life quest, but do as much as you can anyway. Learn about self-esteem and dedicate each week to implement one idea. You can find many ideas in my blog www.ronitbaras.com. Remember, the information is out there, you just have to take it and use it.

✓ Stick out positively – there are good ways and bad ways to stick out. If people are annoyed with you, you are obviously not getting their approval and you are choosing the wrong way to stick out. You can always stick out by being good at what you do and by being kind and considerate. Not only will this attract the right attention, after a while, you will feel good enough about yourself not to care so much what others think.

✓ Listen when you communicate – approval seekers tend to speak more than the people they talk to. When you communicate with others, control your desire to impress and engage mostly in asking questions and listening. Every time you do not tell others what you think of them, every time you do not find faults in what they do, every time you do not put others down, you are one step on your way out of the approval trap.

✓ Be punctual – being chronically late attracts lots of disapproval. Yes, it will give you attention, but the attention will be negative. If you need approval, stick out by being the person who always comes on time, ready for action.

✓ Count your blessings – feeling sorry for yourself to attract attention brings disapproval with it. Every time you are feeling sorry for yourself or thinking of telling others terrible stories to get their attention and make them feel sorry for you, think that no one wants to associate with failures, complainers and losers and they will eventually leave you. Every time you want to say something like that, swap it with a blessing. Instead of saying, "I had the flu and I almost died", say, "I recovered quickly," or "I had a bit of time to rest". There is always a positive way to look at things.

✓ Have a system for making decisions – fear of failure can be really debilitating and wanting to look good to other people can turn people into big procrastinators or perfectionists. Tell yourself, "I will check 3 times and that's it" or "I'll ask one person to read it for feedback and that's it". Editing and improving never ends and the belief that if you improve, you will get more approval is false. At some stage, when you go over a test paper, you start changing things that were correct in the first place. Come up with a rule and stick to it.

✓ When talking about others, only say good things and be honest – when you say bad things about others, you may be doing it because you want them to be perceived as inferior compared to you. The technique is very easy. Every day, say something good about someone. We do it at dinnertime sometimes – we go around the table and say something good to another person. Because people like to build rapport, you will get back what you give, and people will start saying good things about you with no effort on your part.

✓ Learn to be assertive – again, this is a lifelong quest and we all need to be assertiveness artists. When you express your needs without hurting anyone else, you are assertive. "I feel sad and I would like you to treat me with respect" is assertive. "You made me sad because you did… you have to treat me with respect and if not, I will make you suffer" is not. Learning to be assertive will also help you resolve and avoid conflicts and understand that when others think differently, this is not a threat and you can still hold your own thoughts and ideas. If you eat at a restaurant and the food is not hot enough, calmly call the waiter and say, "The food is cold. Please replace it for me". It is not a conflict, because you have paid for hot food and the restaurant takes issues like this into consideration.

✓ Distinguish between being proud and bragging – being proud is saying something good about yourself. Bragging is comparing yourself to others or needing others to be inferior for you to feel good about yourself. Make a list of 100 things you are proud of and read it every day. Remember, you can be good at something without somebody else being not good at it.

✓ Learn and consider yourself smart – smart does not mean achieving academically or having higher education. You can be a smart person even if you left school early (like Einstein was). Being curious and feeding this curiosity will make you a smart person, so develop your curiosity and feed it!

✓ Compliment and reward yourself – we all like compliments and rewards but we do not have to get them from others. We can give them to ourselves. Whenever I achieve something, I reward myself with time off, I buy myself something, I cook something I like to eat, I go for a walk on the beach and so on. I can reward myself any time and by that, I need others to reward me less and less.

✓ Learn how to buy time – when someone asks you to do something and you are not sure, say, "I need to check my schedule", "I need to check with my wife" (This is my husband's secret weapon) or "I'll get back to you on this". This will buy you time until you find the confidence to say "No" or calmly decide to say "Yes".

✓ Be kind – give for the sake of giving without rewards. People in the approval trap give to others only when they expect some reward, but that gets them the opposite of what they want. When they help someone, they seek their approval, but by doing it for the approval and making others feel uncomfortable to have asked for help, they attract disapproval. In this cycle, the other person will ask less and less, and the trapped approval seeker will get fewer and fewer opportunities to get rewards and increase their significance. Be kind for the sake of kindness and for making this world a better place. You will be surprised how good it feels (see my blog post Make a List: Ways to Be Kind).

✓ Have a vision and set goals – with a vision and clear goals, you are less likely to drift towards what other people want in life and more likely to have a good understanding of yourself. Only 10% of the people in modern society have goals. Not surprisingly, these are the most successful people. You can find lots of information regarding goal setting on my blog. Write a goal for every area of your life for the next 3 months, 1 year, 5 years and 10 years.

✓ Consider your compromises – life is full of compromises. When you make a decision, take a minute to think clearly and independently and ask yourself "This is what I gain from doing it, but what am I going to lose?" Then, weigh the benefits and losses for the short term and long term. Never ever lose more than you gain!

✓ Choose when to zig and when to zag – the choice whether to stick out or follow the herd must be done when you are not stressed. We cannot always stick out or always follow the herd and when you make the choice calmly, you have much more control over your life. Remember to become a leader of your family, you require followers (your kids). Most leaders are "Zaggers".

- ✓ Live and let live – what others do to look good or bad is none of your business. You are not there to tell them what to do or how to do it. On the other hand, your need for approval is your problem, so do not make it theirs. What you think and do is your choice and you do not need others to think and do the same in order to be convinced that you have made the right choice. Do what you think is right for you and allow others to make their own choices.

- ✓ Notice when you control others or put them down – every time you put someone else down, or try to control them, you send a message to your subconscious that you are projecting low self-esteem. Find out what triggers this behavior, catch yourself when you do it and build your self-esteem with acceptance and encouragement.

- ✓ Leadership skills – not everyone is born a leader, but to be a successful leader of your family for example, means that you have developed independent and critical thinking. To find out how leaders think, find leaders that inspire you (teachers, friends, your own parents or someone else that has followers) and learn what they do that makes others follow them. You will never find a leader who lives without vision and goals or takes ages to make a decision. Learn from other leaders by associating with them or by reading about them – the library is full of books about leaders.

- ✓ Take some time with yourself – fear of being on your own can draw you into the trap of approval by compromising your relationship needs and thinking that it is better to be with someone who abuses you just to avoid the pain of being on your own. Find 15 minutes every week to be by yourself and gradually increase that time. Do some fun things in your "me time", enjoy your own company and learn to be independent.

Like many others, my client, Talia, had a very particular trap of wanting to please one person – her mom. In the process, she learned that she was giving her mom power her mom never had or wanted (after she left home). By implementing each of the tips mentioned here, she got out of the trap into a very happy and fulfilled life. If I thought she was a successful and inspiring person before, you can imagine how much more she

could do after our coaching and how happy she was with herself and with her mom.

 Stop looking outside for scraps of pleasure of fulfillment, for validation, security, or love — you have treasure within that infinitely greater than anything the world can offer.

— Eckhart Tolle

If you want to motivate your kids, never use the approval as a parenting tool. Kindness, acceptance and being a role model, can do lots more.

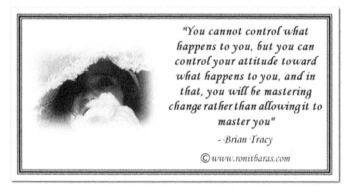

"You cannot control what happens to you, but you can control your attitude toward what happens to you, and in that, you will be mastering change rather than allowing it to master you"

- Brian Tracy

© www.ronitbaras.com

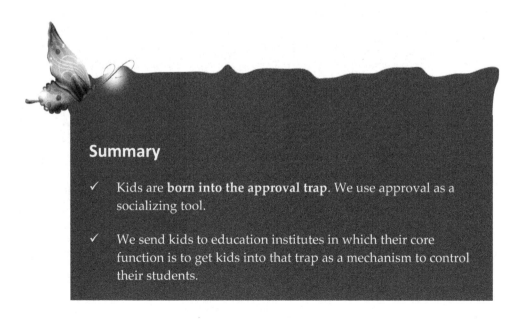

Summary

✓ Kids are **born into the approval trap**. We use approval as a socializing tool.

✓ We send kids to education institutes in which their core function is to get kids into that trap as a mechanism to control their students.

✓ It is hard to motivate someone in the approval trap, as he will tend to go where there is more pressure. If you raise kids using approval as a parenting tool, you **sentence your kid to be easily pressured by disapproval**.

✓ Approval is a drug and parents are the drug dealers.

✓ **Parents in the approval trap raise kids in the approval trap** who will raise their kids in the approval trap. **Every parent has the power to stop the cycle.** Reflect on your need for power, accept your own parents, yourself and be the one to make the change and be the change you want to see.

✓ People who are trapped have specific **character traits and use specific vocabulary**. They are followers who seek permission, and significance, put others before themselves, blame others, are easily pressured, jealous, afraid, competitive and not assertive.

✓ There are **25 strategies to get out of the approval trap**. Developing critical thinking, developing responsible attitude, practicing independent thinking, associating with the right crowd, developing a sense of uniqueness, building self-esteem, sticking out positively, listening, being punctual, counting your blessings, having a system to make decisions, saying good things about others and being honest, learning assertiveness, being proud not bragging, thinking of yourself as smart, complimenting and rewarding yourself, mastering time management, being kind, having visions and setting goals, considering compromises, evaluating when to zig and when to zag, living and letting live, noticing a desire to control or put others down, developing leadership skills, dedicating time to be with yourself. Each of the strategies can make the shift by itself. All you have to do is try them, one by one until you feel your need for approval is not so big. Once you are free from this "drug", it is time to set your kids free as well.

PRAISE AND APPRECIATION

Praise and appreciation are carrot-type motivators that work easily and create long lasting effects. It is a good idea to understand the dynamic of praise in order to be able to use it wisely.

The question of praising kids has been discussed for many years among educators and psychologists. While in the old days, parents did not compliment their kids so they would not think too highly of themselves and be humble, a new age started when praising and complimenting kids was highly recommended by the experts.

Well, which of these approaches has survived the test of reality? Which of them produces "better" or more successful kids?

Try to guess before you go on reading.

Smart is confident. Not!

Many parents think that focusing on their kids' academic achievements and making them "smart" is the right formula for success and confidence.

But if the kids do not know they are smart, how will that build up their confidence?

Kids know they are smart, because someone tells them they are. According to a survey conducted by Columbia University, 85 percent of American parents think it is important to tell their kids they are smart.

A research on kids' confidence and intelligence has discovered that smart kids who are aware of their intelligence do not always translate their academic abilities into emotional strength. Kids who scored extremely high on their IQ tests and were praised for their "smartness" were less likely to try new tasks that seemed hard for them.

To a smart child with the capacity to learn quickly and easily, tasks are split into two categories: the things I can do without effort (and I am sure to get right) and the things that may be too hard for me. So, they do the easy things and go to great lengths to avoid the hard ones in order to maintain their confidence.

The sad news is that too many of the gifted kids who are aware of their cleverness fail to appreciate their abilities enough and have low expectations from themselves, so they need more help than "normal" kids do.

Strange, right?

Well, let me tell you how this happens.

Professor Carol Dweck researched the effect of praising for 10 years on 400 5th Grade students at 12 schools in New York. She concluded that praise can be dangerous. Her research about praising kids has found that telling kids they were smart did not guarantee high performance. It was more likely to cause low performance!

In the first stage, researchers asked each child to complete a simple non-verbal IQ test with very easy puzzles. Once the kids finished, the researcher gave them their score and praised them. Regardless of their score, one group of kids were praised for their intelligence by saying, *"You must be smart at this"* and the other group was praised for their effort by saying, *"You must have worked really hard"*.

In the second stage, the same kids were given a choice to participate in a second round of tests, but this time, they could choose the test in which to participate. They had to choose between a test that was more difficult than the previous and one that was easier. To encourage the kids to take the hard test, the researcher told the kids they had learned a lot from attempting the first puzzle. 90% of those who had been praised for effort chose the difficult test. Most of the kids who had been praised for being smart chose the **easy** test.

In the third stage of the research, Professor Dweck gave the kids a test that was designed for kids in 7th Grade (2 years older). The kids who had been praised for effort made more attempts to complete the test, while those who had been praised for being smart thought they were failing simply because they were not smart enough and stopped trying.

Did you know?

Research found that kids who scored extremely high on their IQ tests and were praised for their "smartness" were less likely to try new tasks that seemed hard for them. Praise for effort!

In the fourth stage, Professor Dweck gave the kids a test that was as simple as the first one. On average, those who had been praised for their effort **scored 30% higher**. Those who had been praised for being smart **scored on average about 20% lower.**

Kids who are praised for effort have a feeling they can control their level of success by doing more work or spending more time, so they do as much as they can. Kids who are praised for being smart believe their cleverness is an inherent ability over which they have no control, so they quickly assess their chances of success and when things appear to be too hard, they simply give up.

In case you were wondering about the effects of age and gender on this research, Prof. Dweck has found the same results for boys and girls and for kids of all ages, including pre-school children.

The above research results were amazing, because the self-esteem "movement" had claimed that praises were essential in establishing self-esteem in kids and supported giving kids the "belief" they were smart. I agree. It is essential to praise … effort!

The Appreciation Bowl

The good thing about praise and appreciation is that they are free and do not require any preparation or special set up.

Kids will do a lot for a kind word from their parents. This is so important, I know many grownups who have dedicated their life to making their parents say "one good thing" about them.

The simplest way to use praise for motivation is to say good things about your **kids every day for every little thing**. Unfortunately, we tend to say things when our kids do not do what we expect of them and by that, we reinforce the things we wish to eliminate.

Imagine that your kids have a "**praise and appreciation bowl**". When it is full, you can motivate them to do anything, but when it is empty, it will be a challenge to motivate them to do even the smallest things. In some psychological theories, confidence is highly connected to this "appreciation bowl".

At the beginning of their lives, kids highly depend on their parents or other family members to fill up this appreciation bowl. When they start leaving home and spend time with other socializing agents like day care providers, teachers, hobby facilitators, coaches, they still depend on others to fill in their bowl. Why? Because as young kids, they don't know how to comfort themselves, encourage or motivate themselves. They develop this mindset *"I am good **only if** others say I am good"* and school is not very helping in that sense with the use of testing and marking. Many children grow up not learning how to fill in their own appreciation bowl and depend highly on others to highlight successful experiences and fill up this bowl, which is again, the Approval Trap.

Many parents ask me "how much praise is enough to fill up the bowl" and my answer is "every kid has a different sized bowl and unfortunately, the less praise they get, the bigger it seems, and they have a greater need for praise to make them feel confident. Criticism, judgment, anger, disappointment, pressure, threats and fear depletes this bowl so in a sense it is never completely full. If you want to have a formula for a fuller bowl, **reward every attempt and praise it, regardless of the outcome**".

Kids brains, much like adult brains, record every event as a "happy, successful" event or "a sad or failure" event (or versions of the same thing). If we want to direct our kids to do things, we need to make sure that what we want to encourage them to do will be registered as a "happy, successful" event regardless of the outcome. Here, I will say it again, if we want kids to do something over and over again, we need them to register this behavior as a "happy and successful event" instead of registering a "sad or failure" event (which often is registered by criticizing, showing you are disappointed, threatening, fear, judgment, patronizing or anger.

  One praise a day will go a long way

         – Ronit Baras

Here is an example of something that happened in our house.

During one of the school breaks, when my son was 13-year-old, he was chosen to participate in a special 4-day program for young musicians at the Griffith University Conservatorium. He was in a special choir with 76 other talented kids from all over the country and learned many great things about

singing. At the end of the first day of camp, after learning 5 new songs, the conductor told them she would be holding auditions for solo parts in each of the songs and encouraged everyone to participate. Back then, singing was not our son strongest talent (he was mainly a percussionist and a composer), but he auditioned for two of the songs in his voice range. In the evening, he told us about the whole day and said many kids who had auditioned had voices much better than his. He seemed really worried that others were singing so beautifully. *"I will know tomorrow if I was successful or not"*, he said as he went to bed.

Gal and I looked at each other, smiling. We knew that it was a great opportunity to make the event, that seemed stressful for him a "happy and successful" one so we followed him to his room and said, *"You do not need to wait for tomorrow. To us, you have already succeeded"*.

He looked up at us smiling, not sure what we meant, and I thought that was the most wonderful opportunity to tell him the story about the **lottery ticket.**

In my leadership camps, workshops and presentations, I share the Lottery ticket story and I think it is a useful tool in the parenting/ managing/ motivating/ coaching tool kit. I hope you will make good use of this story as much as I did. I say, if you hear yourself sharing this story the third time, it means it is integral part of your tool kit.

The Lottery Ticket

A religious Jew went every Friday to the Wailing Wall in Jerusalem and put a little note with a request from God. Every Friday for 30 years, he asked the same thing – *"God, please let me win the lottery"*. Every time, he wrote about all the wonderful things he would do if God let  him win the Lottery, most of which was giving to charity and making the world a better place.

The angel who collects the notes from the wall became fond of the old "lottery man" and after so many years, decided to go and speak in his favor with God.

"God, this man is a very good man." Said the angel, "He is a man of faith and only wants to do good. It breaks my heart to see him put note after note and not get his wish. Can you please let him win the lottery once?"

God smiled to the angel and said, "I would have, if he only bought a ticket".

As my son heard the story, he smiled. He knew that on the way to succeed, you must take action and "buy a ticket". We knew that for him, auditioning had been hard, because he risked being turned down or being embarrassed, and we told him that regardless of what the conductor would say the next day, auditioning in spite of his fears had been his real success.

[He did get one of the solo parts and was very proud of himself, as were we. This audition started his whole journey in singing, as well as percussion and composing]

> *Be willing to make decisions. That's the most important quality in a good leader. Don't fall victim to what I call the "ready — aim — aim — aim — aim syndrome. You must be willing to fire.*
>
> — T. Boone Pickens

Praising effort gives kids the message that stretching themselves and doing things that are hard for them is the real success in life. In my son's case, the knowledge that even if he did not get a solo in the choir, we would still think he was successful, probably helped him a lot and would have supported him in case he got nothing.

Although this incident turned out to be a successful one, because he is such a talented kid, he needs to face many potential failures. The same year he came back from an Australia-wide competition in Sydney and did not win any prize. He was terribly disappointed and felt even worse when everyone in the competition, including other adjudicators, students and teachers told him he should have won first prize in at least two of his performances.

It took him exactly one day to recover! As he came back to school the following day, he was fully motivated and energetic again. I believe that was partly because when he returned, we told him, *"Getting a prize can be a matter of personal taste. What you have learned in the lead-up to the competition is what makes you a winner, not the prize that someone else gives you. Preparing yourself the best you could and performing the best you could is the real success"*.

Through praising the process and appreciating the real rewards – knowing something new, or doing something we were afraid of – we send a message that life is easier for people, not just kids, when they bounce back from a failure experience and try again and again and again. Success is not the result of a lucky charm, but the ability to bounce back.

The brain motivation switch

Dr. Robert Cloninger from Washington University in St. Louis discovered there is a "switch" in the brain that functions as an internal motivator. When the person does not receive an immediate reward, something kicks in and sends messages like *"Don't give up"*, *"Come on, try again"*, *"There is a dopamine* (the brain chemical that gives us the  feeling of satisfaction and reward*) just around the corner"*. When Cloninger checked people's MRI, he discovered this switch functioned well in some people, but not in others.

You are probably asking yourself, "What about me? Do I have a working switch or not?" or "does my child have it?"

Dr. Cloninger asked himself the same question. He trained rats to run a maze and increase their persistence by not rewarding them every time they reached the finish line. According to his research, the brain learns that frustration can be worked through. *"A person who grows up getting rewards too frequently will not become persistent, because they will quit when the rewards disappear"*, he claims.

Praise junkies

The same works for praising. When praise focuses on the result (like the prize, in the rat experiment) and is too frequent, kids become addicted to it and can no longer survive without it. It may sound funny, but praising only for end results and too frequently lowers kids' ability to motivate themselves and makes them, well, quitters.

Praise is a form of a feedback, which can work to your advantage as a parent or backfire and prevent your kids from developing their built-in chemical reward switch that keeps them moving forward.

Finding the balance

Sometimes, parents are so hooked on success themselves that, they consider cheating by helping their kids look better, get praise and win awards. Teachers can easily recognize this kind of parents when their kids bring a project to school that is so good their mom or dad must have done it all for them.

At every parenting workshop, I am asked about the difference between being pushy and encouraging. Every time, my answer is this:

When you motivate your kids to do something they want,
you are encouraging them.
When you motivate your kids to do something you want,
you are pushing them

- Ronit Baras

To raise successful kids, parents must find the balance between motivating their kids to do their best by praising effort and directing them towards new things through praising with a "hidden agenda". As with anything else, when you overdo it, your kids will catch you and your cause is lost.

Remember, praising is a wonderful tool if you mix in with the right ingredient of encouraging effort to fill up their appreciation bowl and helping the motivation switch stay on.

Parents with empty bowls

The hardest thing to do is to praise kids when your bowl is empty. It is almost like sharing food you don't have yourself. Researchers found out that parents praise their kids when they feel good and "take away "praises when they feel unappreciated themselves.

The reasons parents feel "empty" can vary.

It can be that their own parents or other socializing agents did not fill up their bowls in the critical times of their life.

Or they experience praise as kids but had more criticism, judgment, patronizing, anger or feelings of inadequacy.

It can be because they hang around people at home/work/friends that constantly empty their bowls (energy consumers).

Or they don't have the skills to fill up their own bowl.

Or that they don't think they can fill up their own bowl and require someone else to do it for them.

This situation of empty bowls is one of the main reasons people divorce nowadays. They believe their partners are in charge of filling up their empty bowls and are very disappointed when they discover that no one person, no matter how much this person loves them, can do it on his/her own or effectively enough.

Some parents I coach say to me "my son never says nice thing to me" "She is not appreciative" "I have never heard her saying 'thank you dad for picking me up from soccer' why should I say to her 'thank you for helping with the laundry?'"

Well, in parent-child relationship the parent is the only socializing agent. I know it is tough, but it is part of the parenting job description. You are the parent. Your kid can start praising only when he/she develops some critical thinking and his/her bowl is full.

Here is an example of how to fill a kid's bowl. I have been running leadership camps for years and as part of the camp activities, I ask the parents to write letters to their own kids titled "I believe in you!" Every year, when we get to this stage and I give the kids their surprise letter (sealed and only they can read it) we have two to three hours of tears of joy and sadness.

Why joy?

Joy to read on paper how much they are loved and appreciated.

Why sadness?

Sadness that they hardly ever hear it face to face.

We spend 2-3 hours talking about parent-child relationships, about praise and compliments and how it feels to know that your parent appreciates you. I tell them about my own mom, who had never heard praise that from her mother and how in a very courageous act, she wrote to me that she cared for me and loved me, and how much I cherish those words and the letter she wrote me.

When I ask the kids, *"How do you think your parents would feel if they received something like that from you?"* Most of them feel an urge to write a letter back. After reading the letters their bowl is so full, they are willing to give back.

Let me tell you, holding such a letter in your hands brings lots of emotions. You feel powerful beyond measure and it does not matter how old you are. This is why I have started including the letters in my kids/students coaching activities and 100% of the times, I get emails or meet parents of kids who participated in my activities that claim their child came back from camp/ leadership training/ day activity a different child and they thank me for it. I usually thank them for having the courage to write the letters.

Give and you shall receive, and parents must give first.

Did you know?

Research shows that praising and appreciation can do magic to kids' motivation however, frequent rewards can lead to giving up the second the reward disappears. Do not raise praise junkies and find the balance between praising for achievements and praising for effort.

Exercise

Write a letter to your kids with all the good things you want to say about them and to them. Seal it and give it to them. You can email them or record it but make sure it is in a format they can keep.

It is hard to "give" when you are upset but keeping your focus on promoting the good behavior is the only way to make sure your child will be motivated to do the "right" thing. It is inevitable that your child will do things that make you upset. Don't be tempted to tell him off or "teach him a lesson". Try to find something good to say. I know it is hard but not impossible. Here is an example I had to find something good to say when I was really, really angry.

My daughter Eden was always a great kid and while many friends of mine struggled raising their kids, she has been a very "parent friendly child". One day, when she was about 16, she came home and shared with me something she did with a friend that was really inappropriate.

When she shared it with me, she said it as if she knew it was not the right thing to do and I was so angry and disappointed with her. I wanted to say, *"Eden, I don't believe you did such thing"* (disappointment) *"Eden, How stupid of you"* (judgment and criticism). *"Eden, what would your teachers say about you now? About us?"* (guilt) *"What do I need to do to make sure it won't happen again?"* (and my mind went straight to punishment).

I knew that all my thoughts were taking away thoughts. I could imagine her bowl emptying in seconds. I was so upset, but she knew it was not the right thing; she had her lesson even without me saying anything. I knew that if I said anything like that, I would be promoting the behavior I wishes to avoid. I took a deep breath and asked myself, *"How can I fill up her bowl now?"* I believe in "ask and you shall receive" and the idea came straight to me. I looked at her, still angry, disappointed and upset, and said, *"I am happy you were honest and shared it with me. I know now I can trust you to share with me even the things that are challenging"*. I could see the relief in her face.

Think about it. Even when I was judgmental (and I was), I promoted honesty, sharing and trust. I think you can do that too.

Tips for praising and filling up the appreciation bowl

- ✓ Praise and reward for effort not ability or intelligence

- ✓ **Reward effort**, regardless of the outcome

- ✓ **Fill up your child's appreciation bowl.** If you feel your child's bowl is like a bottomless pit and your praise is not enough, do it anyway. Some kids' bowl is so empty it seems huge. Every praise disappears in the bowl without a trace. Remember, it is still there. You only need to pass a critical quantity. Children's confidence depends on the fullness of this bowl. It is the ratio between what goes in and what comes out. Keep praising and make sure you praise more than take out.

- ✓ **Be sincere.** If you mix honest and dishonest praise, all your praises are ignored

- ✓ **Over-praising is addictive** and promotes dependency and competitiveness – keep raising the bar and praising only from the new minimum upwards

- ✓ **Persistence is the key to success.** Teach your kids that to win life's lucky draw, they must first buy a ticket

- ✓ Find the balance between praising for self-esteem and praising for direction

- ✓ Praise and appreciation are easy to use when you feel happy and appreciated, but are more important when you are not. **When you feel upset, find something good to say anyway.** Focusing on positives can only make you feel better.

✓ In the relationship with your kids, you are the adult, so you need to start regardless of how full or empty your appreciation jar is. **Do not expect praise and appreciation in return for yours.** Your kids' bowls need to be full before they can start giving back. If you need help with your bowl, ask other adults for it (or a professional helper, like a life coach).

✓ If you are not a "praising parent", because you don't know what to say, **make a list of praises and use them when you are stuck on ideas.** I have attached a list of praises below. I suggest you put it in an accessible place to allow you to learn some statements from it. Pick the statements you feel more comfortable with and use them a lot.

✓ Every day, before your kids go to sleep, ask yourself, *"How many times did I praise or appreciate my kids today?"* Make sure your kids do not go to sleep before getting **10 praises a day**. You can kiss them goodnight and tell them great things about themselves or you can write notes and put them in your kids' lunch box, send them an email, text them on their mobile... 10 a day will guarantee their bowl will never be empty.

✓ When you are upset at your kids' behavior, remember that expressing disappointment, anger, judgment, criticism, authority or when thinking punishment, you are taking away from your kids and promoting the behavior you wish to eliminate. *Search for something good to say.* In challenging times, what can you promote instead? I have a rule that says, "find something good to say, if you don't have anything good, shut up!" I find it very useful. Don't promote the undesired behavior.

✓ *Teach your kids to praise and appreciate themselves.* In our family, we have self-praising ceremonies, in which each person says good things about him/herself. At dinnertime, each of us tells about one great thing we did today. When I know my kids are proud of themselves for something, I ask, *"How do you feel about it?"* or *"What do you think about yourself?"* and this prompts them to say good things about themselves.

100 Things to Say to My Daughters

I gave Amanda, one of my parenting clients, an assignment to make a list called "100 things to say to my daughters". I gave her this assignment after she told me that no one ever praised her, and she feels uncomfortable saying those things out loud. The great thing was that Amanda did think her daughters (she had three gorgeous girls) were wonderful but she seemed to highlight only the things they didn't do well and empty their appreciation bowl.

It didn't take long after she completed this list for her home to become a warm and positive place.

(Please note Amanda used some of the praises in her list that were not 100% praising effort, but it still worked)

Use this list for praise and appreciation ideas. You can easily change "girl" to "boy" and "mom" to "dad" to suit yourself.

1.   I am happy you are my daughter

2.   You are so beautiful

3.   I am so happy to see you drawing

4.   You are so smart

5.   That's a good piece of work

6.   You are concentrating very well

7.   Well done!

8.   You are very responsible

9.   You are growing so well

10.   It's great you know what you want

11.   You are very independent

12.   You are cute

13.   You are singing so beautifully

14.   It is good you are positive

15.   Your teacher loves you

16.   It is great that you are persistent

17.   You are such a great helper

18.   You are so good at …

19.   You are playing so nicely together

20.   Your skin is so soft

21.   You have a magic touch

22.   Let's hug. You are my teddy bear

23.   Good job!

24.   You are very mature

25.   Excellent!

26.   It is OK to be upset sometimes

27.   You are my baby

28.   You are friendly

29.   You are wonderful

30.   Everyone loves you

31.   You are playing so nicely with friends

32.   You are getting along so well with your sister

33.   I am proud of you for playing quietly while I am resting

34.   It is great to hear you talking to each other at night, like two fairies

35.   It excites me to see you doing things together

36.   Look at you! You got dressed all by yourself

37.   Thank you for helping me

38.   Your hair is beautiful

39.   I am glad you are trying even when it is hard

40.   Your tummy is soft

41.   You are sweet

42.   You can do it

43.   You make us a happy family

44.   You are very strong

45. It is hard, but I am happy you are not giving up

46. You are such a good girl

47. You are excellent

48. I have fun with you

49. Thank you!

50. You and I grow together. It's wonderful

51. You are fun

52. You are wonderful

53. I am proud that …

54. I appreciate it when …

55. You are the most … girl

56. You make me so happy

57. You are the best thing that ever happened to me

58. You are a good friend

59. To be a wonderful mom, I need wonderful kids and you are a wonderful kid

60. You can do anything you want in life and I will help you do it

61. You have a wonderful smile

62. You have a big heart

63. You are so gentle with your sister

64. You are so considerate

65. I am so proud. I am like a peacock thanks to you

66. You are good

67. I trust you …

68. You are healthy and your body is strong and can heal anything

69. You are special

70. I am the proudest mom in the world

71. If I'm sad, I only need to think about you and my sadness disappears

72. You are brave

73. You are important to me

74. You are my treasure

75. You make me feel like a special mom

76. I can help if you need me

77. You are so joyous

78. You are so happy

79. You have made my day

80. You make me laugh

81. I am happy you are taking good care of yourself

82. It is great that you try different kinds of food

83. You are my sunshine

84. You are the love of my life

85. You can trust yourself

86. I will always help you

87. I will always be here for you

88. You are such a great traveler

89. Just tell me when you need my help

90. I am so happy you are adventurous

91. You are very understanding

92. Everyone thinks highly of you

93. You rock!

94. You dance so beautifully

95. I admire you for …

96. Every mom would love to have a kid like you

97. A girl like you is every mom's dream

98. Being your mom makes me so happy

99. You make parenting so wonderful for me

100. I love you!

Summary

✓ Praise and appreciation are the most basic motivating technique and the easiest

✓ Praises are verbal rewards (I will elaborate on rewards in the next chapter)

✓ Fill up your child's appreciation bowl. If the bowl seems too big, it only means it is empty.

✓ Praise and appreciation do not require a special occasion. *"You eat so cleanly"*, *"Thank you for helping"* and *"I love you"* are good things to say for no reason. In that sense, every day is a special occasion. Any excuse will do.

✓ Kids have a bowl of praises and appreciation that needs to be filled by their parents, family members and teachers. Do not depend on others to do it. You can only control yourself. Keep them away from other socializing agents who "steal" praise and appreciation from their bowl.

✓ In a parent–child relationship, the adult is responsible to start with praises and appreciation. If you need to fill up your bowl, do not expect your child to do it. Get help from a professional person. When your child's bowl is full and they develop critical thinking and some empathy, they will be able to give back and fill up your bowl.

✓ Praise for effort not ability or intelligence. It tends to do the opposite. Smart kids think that intelligence is an ability they are born with and they quit faster if they only think it is hard. Praise effort, regardless of the outcome. Praising the result (the prize) is very risky and promotes "praise Junkies" and "quitters".

✓ Boys and girls need the same appreciation and praise.

✓ Kids need the same appreciation and praise at every age. In fact, even grown up kids need appreciation and praise.

✓ Be sincere. Never tell a child who is struggling in math *"you are a math genius"*. Dishonesty in praising makes your kids ignore you. I have heard too many kids saying, *"Well, she is my mom, every mom thinks her child is the best"* but they don't think of themselves that way.

✓ Do not praise too often. Kids become Praise Junkies and are addicted to the "approval drug". In this approach, they will stop doing what you want them to do the second the "prize" disappears. In other words, if you use conditioning too much, they will start conditioning you.

✓ Praising is a good way to promote persistence. If you want to win in the game of life, you must participate and buy a ticket.

✓ Persistence is a brain function that can be stimulated by rewarding small stretches. Frustration is not the end of the world and preventing it completely may prevent your kid from turning on the *"I can do it if I just keep going"* switch.

✓ Praising for self-esteem and praising for direction are very important but are challenging if the child does not go in the direction you want. Remember that self-esteem is much more important. If they are not on the right track, they need more self-esteem to get out of there. Think of the bowl and even if they are not going in the direction you want, fill up their bowl with self-esteem statements.

✓ Praise and appreciation are easy to use when you feel happy and appreciated, but are more important when you are not. When you feel upset, take time to relax and ask yourself *"what is the good thing I can say now?"* Find something good to say anyway. Focusing on positives can only make you feel better and give you an opportunity to fill up the kid's bowl. What goes around comes around, one day they will praise you back.

✓ Not everyone feels comfortable with praising, especially if you haven't heard it yourself from your socializing agents. It is Ok to use a list to get ideas. Start with 2-3 statements, the rest will follow.

✓ Make sure to praise every day. 10 praises a day will keep trouble away.

✓ The ultimate goal is to help your child praise him/herself so they can fill up their own bowl. Be an example, praise and appreciate yourself out loud so the kids can consider this a legitimate action. Avoid giving your judgment/opinion and ask your kids to evaluate their own work/ thoughts/ideas, you'll be amazed to discover that kids are very honest and accurate in their own self-reflection.

REWARDS

Just like praise and appreciation, rewards are a wonderful way to motivate kids. Based on the "motivation switch" it is very important to understand that rewards are second-level "carrots". Usually, rewards are required when you have exhausted all your praises and they do not seem to work. Sadly, this usually happens when your kids do not trust that you mean what you say.

While praise and appreciation are verbal, kids can keep their rewards with them as long as they want to. It is their way of extending the encouragement and holding on to the thought that you want to make them happy and that you are there to help them move forward.

Rewards are at the heart of Behavior Management and there is an ongoing debate about what a good reward is and what is not so good. Here are my tips on how to get the most out of rewarding your kids and to avoid "side effects".

How to reward your kids

✓ **Kids are different and are motivated by different rewards**. What works for one, does not have to work for others. Your kids are not all the same age and if they are (twins), they are still different kids, so treat them as individuals. If an attempt to use the same reward for all your kids fails (and you would want to start this way to make life easy for yourself), switch to individual rewards.

"The difference between a successful person and others is not a lack of strength, not a lack of knowledge, but rather in a lack of will"
- Vincent J. Lombardi

© www.ronitbaras.com

✓ I would recommend **staying away from food rewards** (especially candy and desserts). A huge portion of our society is obese because they treat food as a reward. No need to add your kids into that group. However, I would consider their favorite meal a good reward and I would make it for the whole family and announce it as a way to celebrate the kids' success. Going out to a restaurant is also a good reward in a family. It combines quality time with doing something special in the same event.

✓ **Prepare a reward list** you feel comfortable with and choose your rewards from it. Never come up with a reward without thinking it through first.

✓ **Discuss the rewards with your partner**. If your kids find that you and your partner disagree on a reward, they will start negotiating with you and you will lose the ability to use this technique to help and encourage your kids.

✓ **Introduce the rewards to your kids in times of peace** and not in time of crisis. Offering a reward after your kids have done something well is encouraging. Offering it on condition of good behavior is bribery. I remember a friend who would say to her 5-year-old son every time we went to a restaurant, *"If you eat your food, you can get ice cream"*. It did not take long before he started saying, *"If you want me to eat, I want my ice cream first"* and nothing helped her. He ate his ice cream first and never ate the food. Do not go there, it is very disempowering. That little boy was scared, because he could not trust his parents' strength of character.

✓ **Never promise what you cannot fulfill** like things you cannot afford, things out of your control, etc. If your word means nothing, you are not providing good support for your kids.

✓ **Match the reward to the kids' age**. Start small. The younger the kids, the happier and more encouraged they are with simple rewards (I can do magic with balloons for 3-4 years old). You have plenty of time for substantial rewards later…

✓ **Alternate rewards**. I have found that some of my rewards lasted for a week, two or three weeks and when the motivation dropped, I needed to use something else. Be flexible and observant.

✓ Introduce **rewards for effort and improvement.** Your kids do not have to be perfect in order to be rewarded. When your kids fail to be perfect (only because they are human), they give up, which is the opposite of what you want. Progress, persistence and commitment are excellent reasons for encouragement.

✓ **Teach your kids to reward themselves**. Help them make a list of things they love doing and things that will make them happy and encourage them to reward themselves. Self-rewards are a good way to guarantee your kids will be able to motivate themselves in the future.

Exercise

Sit down with your kids and help them make a **happy list**. This list can be a great resource for you to use for reward ideas and an excellent resource for your kids to use when they need to encourage themselves. Remember, everything you ask them to do will be easier if you do it yourself. In teaching, we have a rule of experiencing things ourselves to have a better understanding of what kids needs to go through when learning a new concept.

Here are some topics you can mention to your kids to help them fill in their list: hobbies, small gifts, good use of spare time, food, drink, fruit, places to go, friends to visit, things to do with Mom and Dad…

How to make the list of happy things

1. Encourage your kids to write 100 things that make them happy. It might take time, but they will go through several phases and eventually finish.

2. Encourage them to write responsible things – things that are within their power to do or to get. They should avoid things like *"The teacher will give me…"* and *"Kids will invite me…"* as they are not responsible.

3. Encourage them to write simple things that can make them happy without having to spend too much money. Kids need to learn that happiness is free.

4. Work on your list together. It will give you an opportunity to swap ideas.

5.   Encourage your kids to post the list in a visible place to allow them to read it every day and allow you to get ideas to reward them.

6.   Explain to your kids that the list is flexible. Over time, we change our desires and it is perfectly fine and recommended to revisit the list, add, change or remove items from it. The more (relevant) items they have, the happier their life will be.

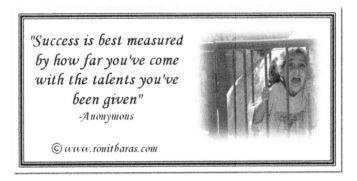

"Success is best measured by how far you've come with the talents you've been given"
-Anonymous

© www.ronitbaras.com

Did you know?

Research on happiness and its cause found that focusing on what makes people happy increase happiness without changing anything else. Participants in the research were asked to write a "success journal" which made them focus on what went well with their day and felt much happier within three weeks. Remember, happiness is a choice! Chose to focus on what make you happy and it will increase your happiness.

Here is a list of rewards to use when you want to motivate your kids to move towards something they want. I have written a list of 100 rewards that are suitable for different ages. Note that many of the pre-school ideas are perfectly suitable for primary-age kids or teens. Temporary tattoos and takeaway foods are wonderful both at age 5 and at age 15. You'll be surprised how useful a smiley sticker is for university students.

100 reward ideas for different ages

Pre-school children

1.   Balloons

2.   Stickers

3.   Party accessories – whistle, rattle, party hat…

4.   Play time with a friend

5.   Sleep over at a friends' house

6.   Inviting a friend to a sleep over

7.   Story time in the library

8.   Shopping with a parent

9.   Special time with mom and dad riding a bike

10.   Special time with mom and dad walking hand in hand

11.   Cooking together

12.   Having a tea party with mom and dad in the garden

13.   Going camping

14.   Traveling

15.   Bringing a takeaway dinner

16.   Going out for dinner/lunch

17.   Their favorite dessert

18.   Camping in the yard or in the living room

19.   Craft activities

20.   Coloring in books

21.   Favorite character socks

22.   Favorite character underwear

23.   Books

24.   Bookmarks

25.   Puzzles

26.   Crayons

27.   Games

28.   Bath toy

29.   Special colorful bubble bath

30.   Sticker tattoos

31.   Pillow fight

32.   Stamps

33.   Bringing a mattress and sleep over with mom and dad

34.   Making music and/or singing

35.   Making a puppet show

36.   Dressing up

37.   Playing with dough

38.   Picnic

39.   An afternoon at the library

40.   Fishing trip

41.   Planting in the garden

42.   Rides in an amusement park

43.   Swimming day

44.   Own make up for games

45.   Picking own birthday theme

46.   Piggy bank

47.   Treasure box

Primary school

1.   Having their own email address

2.   Buying lunch at the cafeteria in school

3.   Novelty diary

4.   Novelty pencil

5.   Novelty pens

6.   Novelty stationery

7.   Glittered pens, papers…

8.   Modeling clay

9.   Chalks

10.   Playing a musical instrument

11.   Sitting in the front seat of the car

12.   Choosing the menu for dinner

13.   Certificates

14.   Pick out the restaurant to go to

15.   Decorate your own room

16.   Skate boarding

17.   Pocket money

18.   Hair accessories

19.   Bowling time with parents or friends

20.   Day off from school to spend with mom or dad

21.   Staying away from home with one of the parents

22.   Having a party at home

23.   Getting their own house keys

24.   Getting their own room

"Trust yourself. You know more than you think you do"
- Benjamin Spock

© www.ronitbaras.com

Teenage/High school

1.   Computer time

2.   TV time

3.   Choosing a movie to watch (together)

4.   Getting their own smartphone

5.   Credit on mobile phone

6.   Privileges for hobbies

7.   Having a part time job

8.   Car privileges when able to drive

9.   Staying up late

10. Dating privileges

11. Special hair cut

12. Inviting friends for dinner

13. Going to a concert

14. Going to the movies

15. Listening to own music

16. Having their own bank account

17. Subscribing to a magazine

18. Coffee or a restaurant with mom or dad

19. Perfumes/aftershave/deodorants

20.   Hair wax for styling

21.   Jewelry

22.   A voucher for iTunes or their own Spotify subscription

23.   Being in charge of organizing a family event

24.   Having friends over for a movie or get together

25.   Gift voucher

26.   Holiday with far away family on your own

27.   Participating in youth related activities

28.   Tools for their hobby

29.   Computer accessories

30.   Personal iPad/tablet

"Really great people make you feel that you, too, can become great"

- Mark Twain

© www.ronitbaras.com

Using privileges as rewards

Privileges are a great way to reward kids and motivate them. Here are tips that will allow you to use privilege rewards successfully and function as a great motivator for your kids.

Privileges jar – Ask your kids to write a list of privileges they would like to have (you will be surprised to read what they write). Give each of your kids small notes of a different color for this. Read all of them and leave only the ones you agree to give them. Fold the notes and put them in a jar. Whenever you want to reward your kids, ask them to pick one of their folded notes from the jar (they can tell by the color) and give them the privilege written on it.

Time with parents is a great reward. Individual time is worth even more. Ask your kids to give themselves rewards of spending time with you. You will be surprised to discover how much they want to spend time with you and the things they want to do. If they take part in rewarding themselves, they learn to motivate themselves.

Summary

✓ Rewards are a great technique to motivate kids. **Use them but never abuse them** and alternate them so your kids do not get used to them.

✓ Rewards are appropriate regardless of the outcome. If you reward success only, it is a formula to de-motivate. **Reward progress and participation**.

✓ It is better to **think ahead of a reward list**. Ask your kids for help; agree with your partner and promise only what you can deliver.

✓ **Never use food as rewards** though outings and eating together can be a good substitute for it.

✓ Kids are different and need different rewards. Adjust the award to the appropriate age and character of the child.

✓ Privileges are great rewards

✓ Always aim to teach your kids to **reward themselves.**

Fall down seven times,
Get up eight

EMOTIONAL STRETCH

Success depends on the ability to move forward and requires persistence. We succeed at school, at work, in our social life, in our parenting, relationships, love life, finances and health only if we can keep moving forward in spite any setbacks.

The movie "Touching the Void" takes this concept of moving forward, no matter what happens, to the extreme of a life and death situation, without the option of failure. There is a beautiful Zen saying defining success as "Fall 7 times. Get up 8". Successful people do not fail less. They get up more.

Kids who learn to persist at an early age just keep going and going and going…

Welcome challenges!

Challenges will always be there. Some say we summon them into our life to prove to ourselves that we are strong and able and to give us perspective. With every challenge, you have the opportunity to strengthen good beliefs about yourself, beliefs that you are capable, that you are strong, that you can and that you are determined. **Welcome challenges! They build self-confidence.**

"Little by little one walks far"
- Peruvian Proverb
© www.ronitbaras.com

Kids are masters at the art of pushing themselves just a little bit more. Just look at them trying to stand up the first time. Whereas they naturally push the boundaries, adults will tighten them. Before they go to bed, if they want more of your attention, they will say, *"I want to stay up just a little bit more. Read me just one more story"*. If you think about it, this is a very wise and positive way to get what they want.

On the other hand, when adults need attention from someone else, they will lower their expectations to avoid failure experiences. It's Funny, but if you want to be able to motivate your kids, you need to go back to feeling like a kid.

Emotional intelligence research has found that kids' ability to persist in spite of the obstacles reaches its peak at the age of 5 and starts declining from there. When given an impossible task, 5-year-olds made an average of 16 attempts to do it anyway. For them, effort was the only key to success (*"If only I try this enough time, I will succeed"*), while 9-year-olds tried only 11 times and 16-year-olds refused to even try, saying it was … impossible. It takes only 11 years to kill our inherent persistence, and when we grow up and start our personal growth journey, we need to re-learn what a natural and healthy ability was.

 Do not confuse motion and progress. A rocking horse keeps moving but does not make any progress.

— Alfred A. Montapert

To motivate your kids, it is important to use their natural attitude towards obstacles. Start when they are young. It will make it a lot easier to motivate them.

Another thing you can do is to slow down the process of giving up by encouraging effort. If the aim is not just to succeed but to keep going, your kids are more likely to keep going.

Whenever I work with kids in special education who are labeled as "hyperactive" or as having ADD or ADHD, I can confidently change the diagnosis only by using the "just a little bit more" technique.

The power of one more second

One of "my famous kids" was a 2-year-old boy Matt, who was brought by his mother to an assessment in my childcare center. I usually write down how long it takes kids to stay in each activity and Matt's attention span was about 5 seconds! He moved from one activity to the next so quickly, I hardly had time to notice what he did. He was like a little tornado.

His mother was desperate and said his siblings had difficulties too and she was very concerned about his development, since he did not talk clearly and could not stay in one place long enough to absorb new information. Matt was the most "hyperactive" child I had ever seen, but I knew it did not matter where I started, it only mattered how dedicated I was to the progress, so I said to her, *"Give me 3 weeks and he will be all right"*.

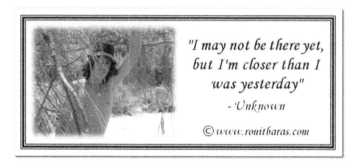

"I may not be there yet, but I'm closer than I was yesterday"
- Unknown

© www.ronitbaras.com

Every day, I worked with Matt on a few activities. Sure enough, 5 seconds after we started, he tried to leave, but I held his hand and asked him a question to keep him just a while longer. When he could sit for 10 seconds and wanted to get up, I held his hand and said, *"Can you help me pack this up?"* After 3 days, he was like a strong wind, but no longer a tornado. His mother said after a week he did not move as much anymore.

Every time I worked with him, I wrote on my chart: 25 seconds, 54 seconds, 3 minutes… People thought it was funny to count seconds, but I am a great believer in "Just a little bit more" and I used it with Matt until he reached what I thought was the best attention span for a 2-year-old – 15 minutes! Yes, 15 minutes, which was a total of 900 seconds.

It did not take a year. Not even a few months. All it took was 3 weeks and Matt was able to concentrate for 15 minutes. When kids move from one activity to another, every 5 seconds, it is very hard for us, as grownups, to notice their abilities. A month later, we found out he had phenomenal visual memory when he also started recognizing words.

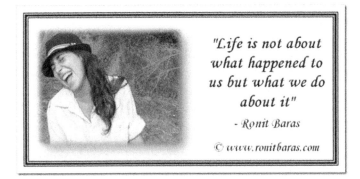

"Life is not about what happened to us but what we do about it"

- Ronit Baras

© www.ronitbaras.com

Matt came with a pacifier in his mouth and could not speak properly, yet within 2 months, he became a different child. When people ask me how I did it, I tell them, *"By counting seconds and being dedicated to 'Just a little bit more'"*. This "little kid" is now a 26-year-old person finishing his degree. He calls me on Skype from time to time and every time I meet his mom, who is a doctor, she thanks me for it. I tell her that I didn't make him who he was, I only used my "one more second" tool to slow him down and allow us all to recognize the warmth beneath the speedy wind.

When you want to encourage your kids to change or make progress, use the "one more" strategy. Kids understand when you tell them success is made up of single achievements, small steps that gradually reach critical mass and tip the balance from effort to success. They understand it because this is how they learn. They experience it every day; they just don't know how to explain it.

Did you know?

Emotional intelligence research has found that kids' ability to persist in spite of the obstacles reaches its peak at the age of 5. Kids are born with inherent persistence. Some call it "stubbornness", but it is in fact, a very healthy and important skill they need in life. If your kids are stubborn, think of it as an opportunity to practice persistence.

> *Kids understand when you tell them success is made up of single achievements, small steps that gradually reach critical mass and tip the balance from effort to success. They understand it because this is how they learn.*
>
> – Ronit Baras

Exercise

Think of things that if you help your kids do just a little bit more you will be able to improve their achievements – school, friends, time management, health, relationships, money, cleaning, organizing…

Just a few more tips

Here is a list of ideas to practice yourself that will allow you to put across the idea of "a little bit more":

When your kids are **sad or disappointed** (or, God forbid, depressed), encourage them to laugh just a little bit more. All they need is one more opportunity to smile about something. The accumulation of smiles and laughs brings more happiness.

When your kids face a **communication conflict**, encourage them to stay in the conversation just a little bit more. Tell them to take a deep breath and show just a little bit more understanding to receive just a little bit more of it in return.

When your kids want **more love in their life**, encourage them to express their love to their parents, siblings and friends just a little bit more than usual. If they say, *"I love you"* once a day, encourage them to say it one more time.

When your kids face **eating problems**, teach them to wait just a little bit longer before piling "seconds" on their plate.

If your kids have **self-esteem challenges**, encourage them to stand in front of the mirror and admire themselves. Every day, they need to stay a little bit longer and notice how their self-confidence changes.

When your kids feel **lonely**, encourage them to hug more. When they hug, teach them to hug just a little bit longer and feel connected.

Whenever your kids **want to feel good about themselves**, encourage them to give a few more compliments to other people. It is a cycle: you give, and you receive. Just a little bit more every day can add up to a wonderful feeling.

When your kids want to **get more rewards from their work**, they need to increase their value every day just a little bit more. They can study something every day, be more efficient, create, improve, innovate and connect. Just a little bit more than yesterday, that is all they need.

When your **kids volunteer their time**, encourage them to volunteer just a little bit more and see that if everyone gives just a little bit more, we all have a lot more. Abundance is everywhere. Giving is receiving.

When your kids **talk with their grandparents**, ask them to show interest, ask one more question and listen a bit more. All they need is to show more interest for their grandparents to reciprocate and express interest more

"Imagination is more important than knowledge"

- Albert Einstein

© www.ronitbaras.com

And maybe the most important tip is to **use all those tips yourself and be an example**. If you are already an example, be more. Show that you stretch yourself and that stretch is a sign of growth.

You may be asking, "How early can kids understand what a stretch is?"

In fact, we are doing it from the second our kids are born. We stretch them with food (when we are not ready, or the food isn't) when they cry at night (and we come a bit later) or when they don't want to go to sleep (and we leave them there anyway). They may not understand it, but they experience it every day and we are the main facilitators of this stretch.

I think they are able to understand it from around the age of three.

Why do I think age three?

"It's kind of fun to do the impossible"
- Walt Disney

© www.ronitbaras.com

Because my daughter understood it at that age, and I have a proof it works. When my youngest daughter was only 3 years old, we counted our emotional stretches for the day every evening at dinnertime. We sat at dinner and everyone had to share something challenging he/she overcame. After a while, listening to others speaking and sharing, she got the gist of it and quickly learned to participate. Her first attempts were "I *wanted to play more but came to help to set the table*" or "I *wanted to have a dessert but kept it to the end*". We knew she understood.

Much research was done on self-regulation and it was found to be highly associated with relationship. **All research indicates that kids who self-regulate are more successful and popular among their friends. As grownups, they have better relationships, are trustworthy and fair, are more profitable in business and less likely to be addicted and have eating disorders**.

"One more" is an important skill in life. Everything that is hard for us to do and we do it anyway is a stretch and a growing experience.

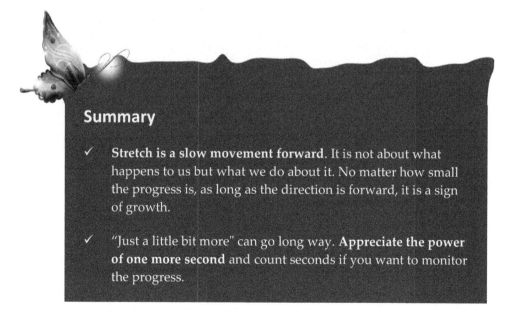

Summary

✓ **Stretch is a slow movement forward**. It is not about what happens to us but what we do about it. No matter how small the progress is, as long as the direction is forward, it is a sign of growth.

✓ "Just a little bit more" can go long way. **Appreciate the power of one more second** and count seconds if you want to monitor the progress.

✓ **Adopt the "just a little bit more" mentality** and encourage your kids to do "just a little bit more" in many aspects of their life. Do not try to do all of them at once. Even rubber bands have a limit to their ability to stretch.

✓ **Children are born with this natural ability to stretch themselves**. It reaches a peak at the age of 5 (we call it the Thomas Edison mentality) and starts declining at the age of 11 until its funeral at the age of 16. This is not a natural process. It is caused by grownups' inability to stretch themselves and be flexible.

✓ **Start early** when they already have some of this ability and encourage it and share your stretches with your kids so you can be a good role model of emotional stretch.

✓ **Motivation is encouraging stretches**. Remember it is painful; this is why it is called stretch. If the child is "torn" it does not mean you have stretched him/her, it means you went too far, and your attempt will be considered forceful and aggressive which can't go hand in hand with motivation. Be gentle, chunk it down and if it didn't work, don't blame the child, chunk it down again.

✓ **Emotional stretch promotes self-regulation**. Self-regulation is like a muscle that needs to be constantly stretched in order to grow, although it is important that this stretching be done by the owner of the muscle and is not by external force. Self-regulation is essential and will give kids the best tool to be successful in life, though remember it is hard to self-regulate on many things at once.

10 CHAPTER TEN

INSPIRATION

One good way to inspire motivation is to use others who have succeeded as role models and try to learn from them. Can you imagine kids growing up to think that many people around them, both younger and older, are sources of inspiration?

 As parents, we are more focused on giving to our kids rather than on teaching them to take

– Ronit Baras

We are constantly giving to our kids. We want to give them knowledge and rules. We want to give them money and support. We want to give them love and wisdom. Instead, we should be teaching them to take understandings and inspiration from the people around them – parents, siblings, grandparents, uncles, aunts, cousins, teachers, friends, their school janitor, their music teacher, their bus driver and the countless other people in their lives.

For most kids, envy is a familiar emotion. It exists from a very young age, as soon as kids must share toys, and intensifies in high school into significant social struggles. Most people consider envy a negative emotion, but, with the help of a powerful motivator, it can be converted into inspiration.

"*The important thing is not to stop questioning. Curiosity has its own reason for existing*"
- *Albert Einstein*
© *www.ronitbaras.com*

Note that inspiring teens is much more challenging than inspiring young children is. Challenging, but not impossible! In other words, start early but do not despair if you are starting when your kids are teens.

It is very important in this process to realize who and what inspires you and it will be much easier for you to inspire your own kids.

Inspiration is contagious. It is an act of giving without the intention of receiving that touches people at their core and helps them move forward towards being better and stronger people. When I take stock of my life: my behavior, my attitude, beliefs and feelings, I often discover that other people have contributed greatly to who I am. When people have contributed in a bad way, I say that because of them or something that happened with them, I got stuck in a bad place in my life. In a sense, I am blaming them for being part of my life. When they have contributed in a good way, I say they have inspired me or encouraged me to reach where I am now. I am grateful and happy that they have been part of my journey.

Early Influencers: Parents and Siblings

It is not by accident that when people see a psychologist to figure out something that bothers them in life, they end up talking about their parents or siblings. These people are major contributors to who we are. Regardless of our relationship with our own families in the present, our parents, brothers and sisters influenced us mainly because of the many years we spend together, often through critical times during our life.

My mom and dad influenced me in different ways, because they were totally different people. As a kid, I had lots of criticism towards them. When I started my personal growth experience at the age of 16 (lucky me, I was young), I changed the question from *"How did they screw up my life?"* to *"How did each of them inspire me?"* It is amazing how many great answers I have received.

My inspiring dad: My dad grew
up in a very chauvinistic society in
Iran, yet my dad is an inspiring
social justice advocate. At home,
he cooked, cleaned, did art and
needlework. He can use a sewing
machine and likes to make silk
scarves. I always thought this was
very special, but when I asked
myself how it had influenced my
life, I realized that I was very

much like him and that he is a wonderful inspiration to me.

My dad inspired me in many ways – I learned from him to work hard, to be
creative and to manage my money well. When I share it with my own kids, I
highlight that focusing on the good things our parents give us, can bring us lots of
joy in life.

My inspiring mom: My mom, on the other hand, is the Chauvinist in the family.
She grew up in a household that thought boys were more important than girls
were, so in our home, she used to give my brother (we were 4 girls and one boy),
discounts in terms of chores at home, while my dad said, *"No, he should wash the
dishes too"*.

So, my mom was not an inspiration when it came to gender equality and social
justice. But she is an inspiration in other areas. My mom never went through a
proper schooling system. She migrated from Iran and left school in 4th Grade. For
years, she had challenges writing and made millions of spelling mistakes.

At the age of 50, she decided to go and complete her schooling. She got it into her
head that if she studied how to read and write, she could get a driving license. She
failed the written test 5 times, but did not give up. She used to sit for hours and
study the signs over and over again. She took 9 driving tests until she passed, and I
still remember the pride on her face when she drove herself to work.

Whenever I think, *"It's too late"* or *"I'm too old for this"*, I remember my inspiring
mom learning to read and write at the age of 50 and I realize it is never too late and
I am never too old.

Did you know?

If motivation is a car, then inspiration is a very clean and efficient fuel to keep it moving forward. You can be inspired by people you know, people you don't know, by people you appreciate and admire. If you are willing to move forward, every person can be an inspiration!

Exercise

Make a list of things that your parents have inspired you to do, think or believe and share them with your own kids.

Big Influencers: Close Relationships

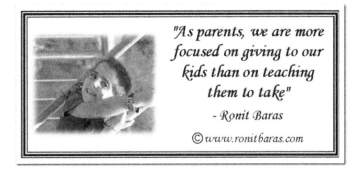

"As parents, we are more focused on giving to our kids than on teaching them to take"

- Ronit Baras

© www.ronitbaras.com

Even if we do not like to admit it, other people in our life have a lot of influence over us. When they are very close to us physically or when we have a strong emotional connection to them, their influence is even greater. Sometimes, it is something they have said, or could never say that defines us. Sometimes, it is something they have done or could never do that affected our life greatly. It could be an experience we have had together that has shaped us. Every interaction has the potential of contributing to our subconscious thoughts and actions and becomes part of the map our "crew" uses to navigate us in the Sea of Life. When we want to motivate our kids to seek inspiration, it is important to understand how we have formed our feelings, thoughts and actions and to identify the people and circumstances that have brought us to where we are because these will be the reasons our kids will form their identity.

When we go through this task of finding those who have influenced us, it is critical to find those who have helped us move forward and those who have "made" us move backwards (I am very careful about the word "made", because I believe they have not done anything to us, but our interaction with them has caused us to go backwards in order to avoid pain). Remember, as long as the final list has more people that have inspired you, you are in a good place.

Sometimes, you can be inspired by someone to move forward, even if the interaction with that person is not pleasant. For example, you have a close family member that experienced something bad (drugs, divorce, betrayal, etc.) and you are inspired not to allow your life to take that path. I have met many people in my life that our close relationship has inspired me to  change, to be strong, to go forward, to try, to take risks and to believe in myself. The close relationship influencers are great additions to your inspiring-person list, and you can search for them in the following groups:

Family – When you think of family, it does not have to be people that are older than you are. They can be younger as well. My own children are an amazing inspiration to me. For example, they all played musical instruments and I had never learned to play a tune in my life. One day, I asked them to teach me how to play the piano. If I thought that playing an instrument was hard, after trying to play piano with two hands, I now admire them even more.

Extended family – It is funny to say, but the person that inspired me the most from my extended family was my mother in law, Gal's mom, who died about 7 years ago. For a major part of my life, she was an inspiration to me. Her life story, her strength and her courage were very important to me. When she died, I felt like something died inside of me with her.

Childhood friends

High school friends

Girlfriends/boyfriends – For me Gal is the biggest boyfriend inspiration. I loved his curiosity and gentleness so much that I wanted my kids to be like that.

Friends from your adult life – One of the friends I had in Singapore was a very colorful woman. While I was very conscious about what I wore or the way I dressed, she used to dress very differently. One day, I asked her why and she asked, *"Why not?"* I realized I did not have a good answer for this. Since then, I have allowed myself to take more risks. When I see someone doing something unusual, I ask myself, "Why not?" and am more accepting of myself and others thanks to her.

Colleagues – In the last 6 years, I have been the state director of a non-profit organization called, Together for Humanity Foundation, which runs cultural diversity programs at schools. This organization is full of inspiring people who are doing something most people avoid doing, because diversity is not an easy subject to deal with. Every person in this organization is an inspiration to me in some way. One of them, Kathleen, was the director before me and the person who introduced me to the organization. Spending about a year with her has changed my life, because many of my ideas about humanity and kindness have changed thanks to her. Kathleen's religion was "Kindness". In some strange way, hanging around her has greatly helped me shape my own philosophy about life.

Family friends

Teachers – It is well known that teachers have a strong influence on most people. If you search all your schooling experiences, you can find the teachers that have left a huge impression on you because of something that has happened between you two. I always say that if you have 3 inspiring teachers in your life, you are a lucky person.

I have a strong negative memory of my 4th Grade teacher who made my life hell in primary school. However, I also remember a teacher and a guidance officer in middle school who helped me a lot and an inspiring teacher, who never taught me personally, but was in charge of our school council when I was in it in 11th and 12th Grade. I had one teacher who taught me that good teachers can even teach physics to people who fail physics (having failed this subject, I had 7 lessons with her and got 94% on my physics exam). I consider myself lucky, because during my special education studies, I had 5 of the most inspiring teachers in the world. Two of them were math teachers, one was a psychologist, one was the head of the Special Education department and one was my Special Education mentor for a year. I know exactly how each of them contributed to who I am today.

Neighbors

Bosses – When I worked at an early childhood center in Texas, my boss was an amazing woman I considered as a mentor. I was 27 years old and she was about 20 years older than I was. She was such a kind woman and she loved everything I did. Whenever I had any doubts, she encouraged me to try again. I think that helped me believe bosses are not enemies but enablers.

Other Influencers: Special Strangers

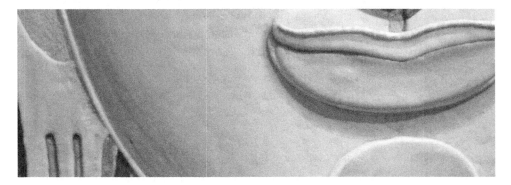

Sometimes, you can be inspired by people you do not know personally, but you hear about them from other sources. It can be a person someone close to you knows, it can be a celebrity or a role model that you do not really know, but reminds you of what you want to be, do or achieve.

I had John Lennon's song "Imagine" written on my wall and the words of the song were carved in my mind. From the age of 16, I have been involved in social justice and in my high school yearbook, when I was asked to write a quote that defined me, I wrote, *"You may say I'm a dreamer, but I am not the only one. Some day you will join us, and the world will be as one"*. I was 18 with no clue that one day I would be the state director of an organization doing just that. My list contains many "strangers" who have inspired me. I never knew Steve Jobs, Walt Disney, the Dalai Lama or Nelson Mandela, but they inspire me still. They do not even have to be alive to inspire me.

 Each of us represents a star in Heaven. Sometimes we shine with the rest, sometimes we twinkle alone and sometimes, when we least expect it, we make someone else's dreams come true

– Unknown

 Exercise

Make a list of all the people you do not know personally but something they have said, done or written has encouraged you or inspired your life. I believe strongly that people come into our life for a reason. Each of them possesses a lesson we need to learn to move forward and grow. If we do not know why someone is in our life, we need to keep searching for the lesson and it will be harder for us to teach our kids to seek inspiration in others. Every person touches us in some strange way and afterwards, we can no longer pretend they were not there, for good or bad. If we take what we can from that relationship, grow and evolve, then regardless of where they are at any given moment, we take them with us everywhere.

Reason, Season or Lifetime

People come into your life for a reason, a season or a lifetime. When you figure out which one it is, you will know what to do for each person. When someone is in your life for a REASON, it is usually to meet a need you have expressed. They have come to assist you through a difficulty; to provide you with guidance and support; to aid you physically, emotionally or spiritually.

They may seem like a godsend, and they are. They are there for the reason you need them to be. Then, without any wrongdoing on your part or at an inconvenient time, this person will say or do something to bring the relationship to an end.

Sometimes they die. Sometimes they walk away. Sometimes they act up and force you to take a stand. What we must realize is that our need has been met, our desire fulfilled; their work is done. The prayer you sent up has been answered and now it is time to move on. It is said that love is blind, but friendship is clairvoyant.

– Unknown

Exercise: Make your own list of inspiring people

- Go over your life from childhood until today and consider all the people you have known

- For every person, ask yourself, "What do I remember about them? How have I been changed by our interaction?"

- For every person, ask yourself, "What do I do, have or believe today as a result of the relationship with this person?"

- Decide if that person has taken you forward or backwards. Remember it is possible that the same person has helped you move forward in one area of life and backwards in another

- When you are done with the list, count and see if you have more forward-moving people in your life or more backwards-moving ones.

- If you can, hang around forward-moving people more. It is likely that your subconscious links them with success, happiness, courage, inspiration and other positive thoughts and feelings, which means you will "allow" them to influence you even more. Do the best you can to be included in your kid's forward moving inspiration list.

 People do not attract that which they want, but that which they are.

– James Allen

1.   If you can, stay away from people who take you backwards

2.	Generally, try to meet new people as often as you can. You never know which one of them will inspire you to do things or be someone you have always wanted to be

3.	Above all, ask yourself if you are carved in someone else's heart as an inspiration. Have you contributed positively to their journey through life, helping them become better, stronger people and an inspiration for others?

> *Treat people as if they were what they ought to be and you help them become what they are capable of being*
>
> – Johann Wolfgang von Goethe

Do not be tempted to do this activity with your child, unless he/she is a teenager. To help your kid, do the following exercises that are more suitable to motivate kids to find their own inspiration or/and shift envy to empowerment.

Exercise: Who's your inspiration?

Ask your kids, *"If you could be anyone you wanted, who would be?"* When you find out 3-4 people they want to be, ask why? The reasons are very important for you to shift your kids from envy to inspiration.

> *Some people come into our lives and quickly go away. Some stay for a while and leave footprints on our hearts. And we are never, ever the same*
>
> – Unknown

What do you find inspiring in others?

If you do know of someone your kids find inspiring, ask them *"What does this person have that you want to have too?"* It is very important to elaborate on the things these kids/people have that your kids may find inspiring. For example:

What **character traits** do they have that help them? Persistence, optimism, determination, courage, friendliness…

What **talents** they do have that help them? Musical ability, knowledge, physical strength, artistic flair…

What **support** do they have that help them? Parents, siblings, family member, coaches, friends…

What **resources do** they have that help them? Computer programs, books, money, outfit, gadgets…

"On the other side of every difficulty lies a new beginning of a better life. You just need to cross over"
- Ronit Baras

© www.ronitbaras.com

Are you inspiring already?

Ask your kids, "In what ways are you already like the person you want to be (like)?"

Envy is a result of kids (and grownups) not realizing their own character traits, talents, support and resources. If you want to be like someone else and hate that person for some reason, then deep inside, in the subconscious mind, the crew that control 90% of what we do, will avoid being like them, so we envy them, but they can't inspire us.

When I run my money mindset workshops, the envy and inspiration always play a huge part in the emotional shift participants go through. We can't have money if we envy those who have money but hate things about them.

I find this question very powerful in all occasions when I want the client (regardless of age or challenge) to use inspiration as a tool. I can offer clients people that they may consider an inspiration, but it is always much better for them to come up with people whom they have a strong emotional connection to, and it doesn't matter if they have a good or bad strong emotional connection to this person.

Asking this question facilitates the transition from envy to inspiration. If they are already like their role models in some ways, it should be easier to be more like them.

Exercise: What inspires you?

Think of **books that may inspire your kids**. Make a list of these books so that you can borrow them next time you go to the library and read them with your kids. If your kids are teens, you can read the books separately and then talk about them. A good example is my book Be Special Be Yourself for Teenagers. It can give you and your teen many hours of conversations about inspirational teens.

Think of **movies that may inspire your kids**. Make a list of these movies so that you can purchase, borrow or download on your TV service and watch them with your kids. I deliberately look for movies "based on real events" watch them with my kids. You can read my blog post Make a List: Inspiring Movies to get started.

I find that the most recent **animated films** can be very inspiring. I watch them with my kids and talk to them about what they can learn from the movie. Watching movies has great educational value for parents and most movies that are appropriately rated, offer some value.

Books and movies allow kids to say, *"I wish I was like this"* or *"I wish I could do that"* more freely, because the characters are not directly involved in their life. This also keeps any subsequent discussion much less emotional.

The based on true movies and books plant the ideas in kids' mind that they can do that too without the need for the parents to say anything.

"Shoot for the moon, Even if you miss, you'll land among the stars"

- Brian Littrell

© www.ronitbaras.com

Tips to promote inspiration

✓ Encourage your kids to **associate** with kids who can inspire them. If they want to have lots of friends, help them get together with friendly kids. If they want to be good in swimming, help them get together with dedicated swimmers and so on.

✓ **Say good things** about the people your kids want to be like, but do not compare. Encourage your kids to be inspired by saying good things about those people. *"Tim played so well today, he is so dedicated and cooperative. He deserved the award today"* or *"Sharon was so funny in the show. She is so talented. It is wonderful that you're friends"*

✓ **Asks the librarian for help** – most librarians have lists of books on the topics you want, and they are very happy to direct you to the exact place in the library.

✓ Share your inspiration list with your kids. Sometimes it gives them ideas they didn't consider before. I like having an inspiration dinner discussion when we share each other's inspirations. It helps kids learn that we can be inspired from many people, young and old, poor or rich, happy and sad, popular or not.

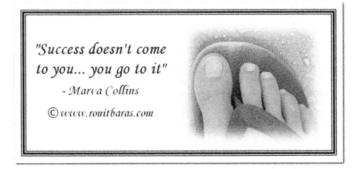

"Success doesn't come to you... you go to it"
- Marva Collins
© www.ronitbaras.com

Exercise: Focus your inspiration and character traits

When you help your kids find inspiration from others, try to **find within you the things you would like your kids to have or be**. If you know what kind of character traits you want your kids to have, it will be easier for you to pick the right people to inspire those things in your kids.

Below there is a list of positive character traits. When you look at them, I am sure you will wish your kids could have all of them.

I know I did the first time I tried it. Unfortunately, it is not easy to focus on all of them, not even in a lifetime, and you have less than 18 years to do it (although we can motivate our kids all our life and sometimes we can be an inspiration for them when we are away, the first 18 years of their life, or the time we spend closely together are the most important for us to build this relationship and influence them.

When they become teenagers, our power over them starts declining mainly because we spend less time together). Therefore, choose only 10 character traits you would most like your kids to have.

 When life gets you down, do you know wanna know what you've gotta do? Just keep swimming!

– Dory from the movie "finding Nemo"

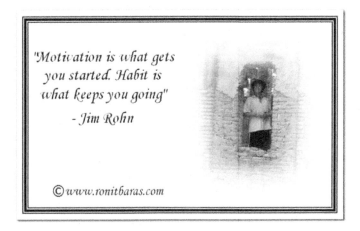

"Motivation is what gets you started. Habit is what keeps you going"
- Jim Rohn

© www.ronitbaras.com

Tips

✓ Think of **traits you have** yourself that will be good for your kids to have as well.

✓ Think **of traits you think you do not have**, but would like to inspire in your kids through other people.

✓ First, tick all the traits you would like your kids to have. Then, combine similar traits. I personally find many of them to be similar, like adaptable and flexible. Finally, narrow down the list by picking the most important, then the next, and so on until you have 10. **Narrowing down** is a good technique to teach your kids as well.

✓ Character traits can be **developed**. Let your kids know they can **choose** to have any quality they want by focusing on it, even if they were not born with it.

✓ If you have **older kids,** show them the list and ask them to **pick their top 10 traits as well**. You may be surprised with the results.

✓ Every person interprets things differently, so it is important to **ensure your definitions match those of your kids**. Ask them what it means for them to be "Brave", "Persistent" and so on. I do that with all my coached kids, and it surprises me every time to find out that what they consider "courageous" is different to my definition.

Positive character traits

Able	Accommodating	Active
Adaptable	Adventurous	Affectionate
Agreeable	Ambitious	Amusing
Appreciative	Approachable	Artistic
Assertive	Attentive	Authoritative
Brave	Bright	Brilliant
Calm	Careful	Cautious
Charismatic	Charming	Cheerful
Clever	Coarse	Compassionate
Confident	Conscientious	Considerate
Consistent	Content	Cooperative
Courageous	Crafty	Creative
Critical	Curious	Daring
Decent	Decisive	Delicate
Determined	Direct	Disciplined
Eager	Easy-Going	Educated
Efficient	Emotional	Empathetic
Encouraging	Energetic	Enthusiastic

Excited	Fair	Faithful
Fearless	Flexible	Focused
Forgiving	Frank	Friendly
Fun-loving	Funny	Gentle
Giving	Glamorous	Good-natured
Graceful	Grateful	Happy
Helpful	Honest	Hopeful
Hospitable	Humble	Humorous
Imaginative	Independent	Insightful
Intelligent	Intuitive	Inventive
Kind	Knowledgeable	Leader
Lively	Logical	Loving
Loyal	Lucky	Macho
Mature	Modest	Nice
Noble	Obedient	Observant
Open-minded	Opinionated	Opportunistic
Optimistic	Organized	Outgoing
Outspoken	Passionate	Patient
Peaceful	Perceptive	Persistent

Persuasive	Philanthropic	Pleasant
Polite	Popular	Positive
Practical	Precise	Proud
Quick	Quiet	Rational
Rational	Rebellious	Reliable
Religious	Resilient	Respectful
Responsible	Romantic	Savvy
Selfless	Sensitive	Sensual
Sentimental	Serious	Sharp
Simple	Sincere	Skillful
Smart	Soft-spoken	Spiritual
Supportive	Sweet	Sympathetic
Tactful	Talented	Talkative
Thankful	Thoughtful	Tolerant
Tough	Trusting	Trustworthy
Useful	Warm	Well-groomed

Summary

✓ **Inspiration is the way to develop self-motivation**. It is like a GPS that can guide us through modeling. Every parent wants to leave in their kids' mind a GPS that will direct them towards success and happiness.

✓ **People can be a great inspiration for all of us.** Go over all the people you have met in your life. Find out how they have contributed to your life by taking you backwards or forward. Find the people who inspired you the most and how they have brought you to where you are today.

✓ People can inspire us by **doing or not doing something** and they can be inspiration to avoid some form of pain.

✓ We can be inspired by people we know directly, by people we know remotely and by strangers. Inspiration is everywhere; we just need to look for it.

✓ Envy can be a source of inspiration – use it! You can use the most important shifting questions:" Who is your inspiration?" "What is inspiring about them?" and help your kids realize what they already have by asking, "Are you inspiring already?"

✓ Help your kids find inspiration in books, movies and friends by encouraging them to read, watch and associate with inspiring kids. Focus on the character traits portrayed in the books and movies and in the friends you want your kids to have.

✓ Say good things about others to model "taking inspiration". It is much easier to be inspired when you have a positive outlook on life.

✓ Share your inspiration list with your kids to give them ideas to legitimize taking inspiration from others.

✓ Pick the **character traits** you would like your kids to have and link them to people who possess those traits. If you are that person, to make sure your kids will be influenced by you, spend more time with them.

✓ Make sure your kids understand that **any character traits can be developed**. Based on Malcolm Gladwell, every person can master any skills with 10,000 hours of practice.

✓ Make sure **your definition matches your child's definition** and please remember that motivating your kids to have a character trait needs to be something they want, not only something you want.

FEAR, FEAR, GO AWAY

Fear is our emotional reaction to something we perceive as a danger. Fear is the most painful stick in the motivation toolkit and unfortunately, it is the most common tool parents use to motivate their kids, mainly because their parents used it and their parent's parents used it…

I believe that using fear is painful and very unhealthy for kids, because the more they fear something, the more important and powerful it becomes. Also, the more afraid they are, the less confident they are and the less internally motivated, which means more fear is needed to get them going. Bad cycle.

Fear is at the heart of every difficulty in life. There is a theory that says there are fundamentally only two feelings: love and fear. Love is all that is considered good and fear is all that is considered bad. If you think about it, frustration, anger, shame, failure and sadness are all forms of fears.

Unfortunately, using fear as a stick breeds many guilty feelings and instead of motivating, it is limiting.

In fact, many times, the reason kids seem to be unmotivated to do something is that they associate this action with something painful. For example, you ask your son to run over to the neighbor and give him some fresh cookies. Although he typically loves to meet people and to be helpful, your son may not be able to communicate that the man next door scares him with his big moustache and rumbling voice. Instead, he may delay, pretend not to hear you or even hide.

Very often, your kids will be afraid of imaginary things, but these will be real enough for them to appear unmotivated. A famous example is children's refusal to go to bed, which leads them to be tired the following day and perform poorly in class, all because of the shadows in the night…As parents, it is important for us to find out what our kids are afraid of. Their fears are their Achilles heel and our task as parents is to help them become immune to arrows (including our arrows).

Tips

✓ Never, never, never use your kids' fears to make them do something.

✓ Never, never, never threaten to use your knowledge of your kid's fears to make them do something.

✓ If you abuse your knowledge of your kids' fears, you will be perceived as the worst bully ever as soon as your kids grow up a bit.

Exercise

Below is a list of fears kids have. See if you can recognize your kids' fears.

Print out the list and go over it together as a family. Each person should highlight or mark the items on the list they fear the most.

Go over each person's top sources of fear and work out the answers to these questions:

What can we do to make sure this won't happen?

What can we do to make you feel better about it?

If your kids are not happy to share their list, let them know they can keep it private and not share or perhaps share only 1-2 items they wish to get your help with.

Reassure them that even grownups have fears by doing the activity with them and sharing some of your fears too. It is important for kids to know mom and dad are human and they also have fears. Also, ask your kids for help with your fears, as this will encourage them to ask for yours.

If your kids do not want to discuss their fears with you, give them the list and say, *"Whenever you are ready and want my help, I will be here to help you"*.

"Courage is being afraid but going on anyhow"
- Dan Rather
© www.ronitbaras.com

Fears kids have (not in order of prevalence)

Fear of shame – an inferior feeling of not fitting with other's standards. This fear is associated with fear of being ridiculed by others.

Fear of getting physically hurt – abuse, accident, sharp objects (knife), falling (elevators, bridges), sickness, death, disasters (earthquake, flood, hurricane).

Fear of public speaking – reading homework at school, speaking at assembly, performing. The fear is associated with fear of imperfection, fear of shame and fear of being ridiculed by others.

Fear of the dark – also fear of the unknown and exposure to movies and books portraying darkness as scary.

Fear of being alone – left out, forgotten, getting lost also connected to fear of being ignored

Fear of supernatural – monsters, bats, demons, ghosts, the number 13, the moon, witches,

Fear of strangers – people they do not know, people looking different like clowns, people behaving differently or speaking differently.

Fear of loud voices – storms, screaming, and shouting.

Fear of first things (fear of the unknown) – first day in school, first sleepover, first camp, first test, first time away from home, first trip to dentist.

Fear of animals – when the fear is non-realistic like fear of spiders, ants or very small insects that cannot really hurt and kids run their life according to it, the fear becomes a phobia.

Fear of scary sights – makes kids remember unpleasant things – blood, horror movies, graveyards, deformed people.

Fear of criticism or disapproval – leads to fear of making decisions and has some fear of failure attached. Typical for kids who are criticized a lot. Usually, kids who fear criticism develop the "disease to please".

Fear or being ignored – challenges in self-expression and low self-esteem in fear from not being acknowledged.

Fear of guilt feeling – belief in superstitions "just in case", perceiving "small risks" as dangerous, challenges in conflicts and having the "disease to please".

Fear of imperfection – perfectionism towards self and others, devastation when not being the "best", competitive mindset.

Fear of big things – sea or ocean, airplane, high-rise building, open space, the sky.

Fear of punishment – high focus on avoidance, on not being caught, on hiding, lying.

Fear of the unknown – forms of anxiety not knowing what the future holds. Those kids will seem procrastinators and paralyzed when trying to make decisions and move forward.

"Champions are willing to do the things they dislike to create something they do like. Don't let the things that matter most be at the mercy of the things that matter least"
- Dexter Yager
© www.ronitbaras.com

It is very important to consider fears as part of life and you can use many of the stories in this book to help them understand that we must participate and take risks if we want to succeed in life.

Never mock or judge a fear and help them understand that time is a great healer and that conquering fears is a huge emotional stretch and a sign of growth. Face the fear in the eye and do it anyway.

I like explaining it like going on a rollercoaster ride. You climb up and the fear starts building up. When you stand up high, the second before you start sliding down, you tell yourself, *"Well, there is nothing I can do now but let go and enjoy the ride down"*.

Most of the time, when kids get down, they immediately go and stand in line for another turn. Life is the same; you are afraid but do it anyway.

Did you know?

Though fear and anxiety seem similar in reactions, they are not the same. Fear is a reaction to real experience and anxiety is a subconscious emotional or physical reaction to a scary thought regarding the future. Anxiety can be triggered without any real danger or threat. When helping your child, distinguish between fear and anxiety.

Sometimes you do all the right things and your kids are scared of things that are out of your control. Still, it is important to help them overcome the fear, because motivating children who are afraid is very hard and complicated. Think of fear as a belief, a thought that prevents us from experiencing pain. Since pain is so strong, our subconscious mind will do everything within its power to avoid it. When I say everything, I mean everything. If you want to motivate kids (or grownups) and they are afraid of something associated with the motivation topic, their subconscious will be on guard and even more sensitive. Remember, the crew is much stronger than the captain is. So, your first goal when dealing with a kid who is afraid is to help your kid overcome the fear or dissociate it with the motivating subject.

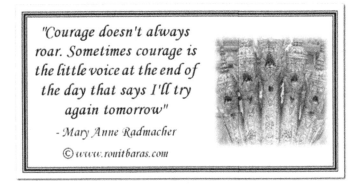

> *"Courage doesn't always roar. Sometimes courage is the little voice at the end of the day that says I'll try again tomorrow"*
>
> *- Mary Anne Radmacher*
>
> © *www.ronitbaras.com*

Here are some tips to help your children overcome their fears.

Tip #1: Watch your buts

If we could record kids' while they experience fear, we could hear a pattern. Most of the self-talk would sound like this:

- I want to express how I feel, **but** I'm afraid they won't listen

- I want to do join this group, **but** I'm afraid of being rejected

- I want to make dad something special, **but** I'm afraid he won't like it

- I want to do my homework, **but** I'm afraid I won't have time to play outside.

- I want to sing, **but** I'm afraid no one will like my voice

As you can see from all these examples, they have a formula:

> I want to <do something>, **but** I'm afraid <of some negative outcome>

This formula is an anchor and kids learn it from the adults in their life. They use this anchor as a defense mechanism to prevent experiencing pain.

What do you think will happen if you change the order?

I want to <do something>. I think <of some negative outcome>, **but** <this is why I'm going to do it anyway>

Here is how their brain will sound once they change the pattern.

- I want to express how I feel. I think they won't listen, **but** my feelings are very important.

- I want to do join this group. I think they will reject me, **but** I have to give it a go,

- I want to make dad something special. I think he won't like it, **but** maybe he will like the thought

- I want to do my homework. I think I won't have time to play outside, **but** if I finish my homework quickly, I'll have plenty of time to play outside.

- I want to sing. I think no one will like my voice, **but** it'll make me happy to sing.

Can you see the difference between the two?

One "makes a big deal" of the situation, while the other is a statement of an option. The first "but" will get kids stuck, while the second "but" will give them more options to investigate the priority/importance and to stretch their creativity.

Teach kids this format and try to use it yourself. We all have to watch our "buts" and in motivation, we can use the "but" to explore more positive options, eliminate fear and do things anyway.

Tip #2: Focus on the want

When your kids are afraid, help them focus on what they want. Remind them what will be the most wonderful outcome of going forward despite the fear. Focusing on the positive outcome is what makes people motivated. It is like telling them to keep their eyes on the target, regardless of the obstacles. I have a family member who is an athlete and a champion, and I give his story as an example of someone that never takes his eyes off the target. There is lots of pain in preparing for a competition but that does not make him want it less.

Tip #3: Bring the wolf

Sometimes, imagining the worst possible outcome can do the trick. Ask them: What will happen if they do not listen? What will happen if you are rejected? What is the worst thing this will actually cause you? Sometimes, when kids play it out in their head, they realize that it is not that painful and that they can manage it. Defining the worst-case scenario is a good technique to realize that the "fear of the wolf is always greater than the wolf itself".

Tip #4: Learn from pain by accepting change

Most kids feel that if something happened in the past, it means it will always happen that way. The fear started at some point in life, yet, they keep it alive through many changes. Help children overcome this belief by finding differences between that first time and now. For example, "I attempted to ride the bike and fell off, so I am afraid to ride the bike" can be changed to "I attempted to ride the bike and fell off but now I am a bit taller and physically stronger". Their brain will try to find similarities to prevent them from the pain of falling off the bike, but it is your responsibility as a parent to break the connections and remind them that every day, with every new experience, they are learning and changing and next time will always, always be different.

Tip #5: Seek alternatives

Many times, fear is the inability to see other options. Help kids think of alternatives. Always ask them to explore another option. Sometimes, when it seems to them that they have exhausted all their options, make sure their parrot says, "I'm sure there is a way and I haven't found it yet!" tell them: "Keep seeking and you will find!"

Tip #6: Seek Inspiration

Help children find inspiration. If they are afraid of doing something, help them find people who have been in the same position and succeeded. Encourage your kids to find how those successful people overcame their fear. This will help your kids overcome their own fears. Many times, knowing that things are possible can help a lot.

Tip #7: Chunking down

Sometimes fear is just being overwhelmed – things seem too hard, too long, too confronting or too complicated. To ease your kid's feeling of being overwhelmed, chunk down the problem into manageable tasks. Chunking down is like "Eating" bite after bite to make it easy to digest. Remember, small steps! Ask them "What can you do today to move forward? What can you do that it is easy? What can you do right now that is within your control?"

Tip#8: Affirmations as reminders

Sometimes forwarding kids to a quote that helps them conquer their fears can do the trick. If you think they are facing specific fears, you can print quotes, put them on the fridge, send them by email or SMS them. If your child is afraid of saying what is important to him/her, you can show him/her this quote:

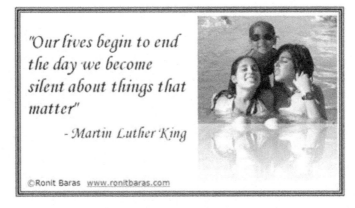

"Our lives begin to end the day we become silent about things that matter"
- Martin Luther King
©Ronit Baras www.ronitbaras.com

If you kids are afraid of not having time, use this statement:

"The bad news is time flies. The good news is you're the pilot"
- Michael Althsuler
©Ronit Baras www.ronitbaras.com

If your child is afraid of what others may think about him/her, use this one:

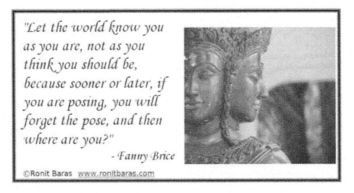

"Let the world know you as you are, not as you think you should be, because sooner or later, if you are posing, you will forget the pose, and then where are you?"
- Fanny Brice
©Ronit Baras www.ronitbaras.com

Remember, you want to help your kids overcome fear and never use it as a motivating tool. In the long run, it is very debilitating, and they associate it with pain.

Summary

✓ Fear is a natural feeling of perceived danger. It does not have to be real or true so don't focus on the validity of the fear. Just focus on how to help.

✓ Kids who are afraid can't be motivated. Fear is not a healthy method to use for motivation. It creates a bad cycle of fear that breeds more fear and makes kids totally paralyzed and unable to make decisions or develop self-motivation. It is a strong action inhibitor and often causes kids to appear unmotivated.

✓ Never, never, never use fear and threats as parenting tools. It will make you the child's bully and the source of your kids' problems. It will only inspire them to stay away from you the second they can be independent.

✓ It helps to discover your kid's fears in order to shift away from any motivating strategy that will raise little victims and to offer help and support to overcome this fear. Many times, finding the source of the fear will help you encourage your kids to stay away from others who take them backwards. Be respectful if they don't want to share and make sure you always say "I'm here if you need me"

✓ Share your fears with your children. It will help them realize it is human to have fears and it is not associated with age or power. When they are young, they look up to you and think you are almighty and strong, if you share fears you legitimize your kids' fears

✓ Help your kids develop healthy ways to deal with their fears by recognizing that conquering them is a sign of emotional stretch and growth. **It is Ok to fear, and it is Ok to conquer it slowly.**

PLANNING & DEADLINES

The bad news is time flies. The good news is you're the pilot.

– Michael Altshuler

Planning is a great motivator for many kids and helps overcome many of the fears they have. When kids learn to plan their time, their actions, their budget, their social life and their activities, they get a sense of control instead of feeling overpowered by external sources.

Planning is another form of chunking down. It is supposed to ease the feeling of being overwhelmed. Many kids want to do things or have things but have no idea how to get them. They do not even know the right questions to ask.

Simple things, like preparing for a test, something most kids experience over and over again during their school years, present time management and technical challenges for kids. Being unable to plan their homework makes it seem hard and may discourage them from even starting.

Do not wait; the time will never be "just right". Start where you stand, and work with whatever tools you may have at your command, and better tools will be found as you go along.

– Napoleon Hill

Research on the relationship between time management and success found that students who did not plan their work achieved less than those who were given detailed deadlines for assignment milestones, and those who had full control over the plan and the deadline, surpassed both group, big time. So, if you want your kid to be motivated to do things, it is much better to teach them time-management skills, planning and how to create their own deadlines, rather than presenting the plan and the deadline for them.

Time management – how to?

Time is a precious thing. Everybody knows that. Although we have had 24 hours every day all our life, it feels like every year we have less of it and the days get shorter, doesn't it? Kids don't have that feeling, they are not very conscious of time and sometimes it gets them into trouble.

It may be hard to accept, but all the people in the world have the same 24 hours each day. Some of them just use it better. People who manage their time well have better control over their lives. **A sense of control is an antidote to fear and is exactly what our kids need in order to feel motivated and confident**.

If you ever tell yourself *"I do not have time"* or *"When I will have the time, I will…"* or *"I wish I had more hours in my day"* you are very normal, but it only means your child needs your help even more.

Why?

Because parents with time management challenges raise kids with time-management challenges. Unfortunately, people are not born with time management skills, but fortunately, they can develop them.

 Nothing is ours except Time

– Goethe

Exercise

The first step in time management is capturing your daily activities at the moment. This step is important in realizing why your time flies and what activities take most of it. It is also very important in scheduling any other activities into your time table.

This activity can be done for adults as well as children as young as 5 years old. With younger kids, I use stickers and magnets to help them develop their understanding of time and to plan (and it works perfectly). I did this activity in class with my students and they learned lots from it.

Make a list of all the things you do in one week. Use an average and do not ignore short 10-minute things, because they add up. People who say, "*Oh, well, it only took 2 minutes*" usually do not control their time well, because they do not realize that 2 minutes + 2 minutes + 2 minutes + … = a lot of time.

When making this list, take into consideration that weekends are not normal days and take into account more sleep and other things you do on the weekend that you do not do during weekdays.

Here are the areas you may consider when making your list:

1.   Sleeping and resting

2.   Working/ going to school

3.   Studying

4.   hobbies

5.   Commuting to work/school

6.   Grooming (shower, shave, make up, getting dressed…)

7.   Shopping

8.   Preparing food (cooking, baking, packing, setting the table)

9.   Eating (breakfast, lunch, dinner)

10.   Cleaning after food (washing dishes, clearing the table, cleaning the kitchen)

11.   Cleaning the house

12.   Laundry (washing, folding, ironing…)

13.　　Watching TV

14.　　Personal email, chat and other personal computer/smart phone time (this, by the way becomes a huge problem for parents nowadays)

15.　　Playing with/without friends

16.　　Going to the doctor

17.　　Studying

18.　　Taking the kids to and from school/activities/friends

19.　　Fun and holiday time

 Those who make the worst of their time most complain about its shortness.

– La Bruyere

When you complete this list, add up all the hours and find out how many hours you spend every week. In each week, there are only 168 hours. Take your sum and deduct it from 168. The result will show you how many spare hours you have every week.

When I give this list to my clients, many of them discover that the accumulation of their activities is more than 168 hours. You are probably wondering how that is possible. Well, it is not! It only means they are chasing their tails and stealing time from themselves.

When kids do that activity, they usually find out that they have lots of spare time and they spend too many hours watching TV or in front of the computer. It is important to show them that some things don't move and don't change and there is no way to save time in those areas (eat, sleep, commute...). If they look at your timetable, it is good for them to appreciate how much of your time is dedicated to them and how much less spare time you have.

If you are one of those who need more than 168 hours, if you want to motivate your kids to control their time, start by controlling yours.

If you have spare time, you will probably notice how little time you have for fun. For kids, fun is what life is all about. It is important to understand that fun is a great motivator for everyone and especially for kids and they will be able to develop some time-management skills if they knew they could have more time for fun.

Did you know?

Research on the relationship between time management and success found out that students who had full control over their study plan and deadlines were much more successful than students who were given detailed deadlines or those who had no study plan at all. If you want to motivate your child to do well in school, help them come up with their own study plan.

Exercise: Time wasters

The second step after discovering where your time flies is to find your **time wasters**. Being skilled in time management means you do not waste time and have habits that make you more focused and effective. If you find your time wasters, you know what areas to focus on. It is very important for kids to find their own time wasters without mom or dad telling them off for wasting time. If you tell them they are wasting time, you are using "force" to make them do something you want. If they read it themselves and understand that everyone has time waters, they develop an internal desire to earn time.

Read the list and spot your challenges. Try to come up with a solution for each of them. At the end, I will write some of my time management tips that are very successful and make you and your child time smart.

This list was developed as a result of a research. The first time waster is the most common one and the tenth time waster is the least common. I found out that every person has a different order. My suggestion is to put them in order of frequency for you. Remember your order is not your child's order.

 Living your life without a plan is like watching television with someone else holding the remote control.

– Peter Turla

Top 10 time wasters

1.   **Shifting priorities** – this happens when you are not sure what is more important, and you react to crises. For people with shifting priorities, pain is the thing that causes the shift and the focus for them is to stop this pain at all costs. Usually, it makes them feel overwhelmed and stressed. Kids change priorities very often due to pressure therefore they are stressed a lot.

2.   **Interruptions** – television, mobile, computer, telephone and people at the door. People often allow external things to mess with their use of time. This usually makes them feel like they are not in control of their time. Kids are highly sensitive to interruptions.

3.   **No clear goals** – not having goals is a habit of reacting to life rather than being able to control some of it. If you do not know what you want, it will take you a lifetime to start travelling, but you will never get anywhere. Kids grow up without goals if they don't learn to have them at home or school.

4.   **Messy desk/room** – on average, it takes people 45 minutes to find a piece of paper. I have many clients who say, *"I can find everything in my mess"*, but in truth, they still have to look for that piece of paper. Ask yourself, *"If something happens to me now and I need my insurance policy, how long will it take me to find it? If I need to track a payment from last year, how long it will take me to find it?"*

5.   **Procrastination** – emotional blocks like boredom, daydreaming, stress, guilt, anger and frustration reduce concentration and cause putting off important jobs. This time waster is very challenging because it drains much energy from people and especially with kids with many fears. Note that doing something efficiently does not make you effective if what you are doing is not the most important thing to do, so look at things you do well too.

6.   **Ineffective delegation** – "Watch out, it comes back". If you want someone to do something for you and you delegate in a way that makes you do it in the end, you have only wasted time. This time waster is not relevant to kids, they never delegate, they load off and throw it on anyone they can.

7.   **Inability to say "No"** – I think this is self-explanatory. Assertiveness is a skill that makes us very effective and focused. If there is something we cannot or do not want to do, it is essential for us to be able to say "No". Kids are not very good with assertiveness and are usually not encouraged to express themselves. From my experience, they will put this one as one of their top problems.

8.   **Poor planning** – not leaving time for routine matters, transit, unforeseen issues (triggers reactive mode) and "downtime" to rejuvenate (which results

in "downtime" due to sickness). Planning takes time, but as we work on our time management skills, we get better at it. Many of my clients think people are either born with it or not, but it takes practice to be effective.

9. **Poor use of technology and systems** – There are many system and gadgets that can save you time. Some people are afraid of systems because they are afraid to lose freedom or that the system will not be 100% bullet proof. The advantage of a system is that after a short time, it becomes a habit and requires less effort than without it. Kids are very flexible with technology but not very good with systems.

10. **Meetings** – 30% of every meeting is a waste of time. If you do not have any need for meetings, lucky you! I learned this many years ago when I worked in a school in Texas and realized that after two full hours, we came out of meetings without making any progress. At the end of every meeting, I asked myself, *"What did we talk about?"* and had no good answer. I asked myself, *"What are we going to do now?"* and had no answer. This is when I learned that when they are not run effectively, meetings are a waste of time. After 2-3 meetings, if I did not have to be there, I did not go.

 The key is in not spending time, but in investing it

– Stephen R. Covey

I learned many of my time management skills during my special education studies. I had so many things to do, it was not human. At one point in my first year of studies, I worked with over 200 kids, had to remember their names, year levels and what academic level each of them was at in order to be able to create an individual program for them. I had to fit in all my study assignments (for 25 subjects I studied every week), homework, quizzes and exams, my work at the Special Education Library, my work and meetings at the Creative Thinking project, library books that were due back at the library within a day, a week, two weeks... and I had to do it well.

It was so overwhelming it was not funny. For a while, I doubted I could do it all, but then I remembered it was not the time we have that counts but how efficient we are with it and I decided to conquer time management. I have learned that when I am busy, I have to come up with better ways to manage the time and I'm much more efficient than when I have all the time in the world.

Even now, more than 30 years later, I am doing lots of things. I coach, I write to magazines, I write my blog, I am a Justice of peace, I do my community work, I teach, I am a director of a not for profit organization, I run workshops, I do my public speaking, I work for the University of Queensland, I run my parenting programs, I share the kids' pickups and drop offs, go to their performances, help them with their activities, cook, clean, volunteer in my daughter's school, do community work, have time for social life, go to the movies with my husband and do all those things and in a very efficient way.

Why?

Because I love variety and because I have to.

> The more business a man has to do, the more he is able to accomplish, for he learns to economize his time.
>
> – Sir Matthew Hale

I myself was a special education kid without any strategies in planning and managing time and my life and my school work looked exactly like that – messy and chaotic. No one could motivate me to do anything. I was so overwhelmed that avoidance was my only strategy. If someone would have told me that one day, I would have a degree in Education and master time, I would have never believed him/her. I use this learning with all the kids I work with, and among my clients, we have a concept called "good busyness".

Time management is very important for me. Since being that overwhelmed during my first year of studies, I have collected tips and ideas to save time and to use time more effectively. I have given those tips to my children and my eldest daughter, who is now 24 years old, is superior to me in her time management skills. Kids who start early, are way more efficient than their parents who start later in life.

I think having the tips was very useful for me and I believe it is one of the easiest strategies to motivate kids because it gives them an immediate advantage and they are very motivated to repeat the success.

 Exercise

Make a list of 100 time-management tips that will make you time smart. You don't need exactly 100 tips but when you search for so many, you reach ideas and places that you wouldn't have searched when looking for 3-4 tips. You may not use all of them today but maybe you can use them when your time is short, or your kids can use some of them.

You can always pick some from my list of time management tips.

Ronit's Time Management Tips

✓ Write **what you already do that saves you time**. It is important to appreciate and keep doing what you do well already.

✓ Ask other people **for time management ideas** – I am in constant search for ideas and I try many of them. Most of my tips come from other people. You don't have to re-invent the wheel.

✓ **Set goals!** Every person must have something he or she wants to do. If you do not know what you want, it will be hard to achieve it…

✓ Find something you do that takes too much of your time and find ways to do it more quickly. **Focus on one thing at a time.**

✓ Think about your day and find a very efficient way to **give yourself another 10 minutes** every morning.

✓ **Have a huge to do list and be very specific.** The longer the "to do" list is, the more efficient you become. To do list only helps you see what you need to do anyway. Seeing it in front of you, makes the prioritizing process more efficient.

✓ Find a diary system/ computer/ app that helps you record your **to-do list and monitor it.**

✓ Use **pencils to write "maybe" things** and pen to write things you can't move if you are using a diary system.

✓ **Use a color-coded system** in your diary and to do list. I use different highlighters for priorities, and it is easy for me to know what I must do first.

✓ Find a filing system that helps you keep your paperwork in an **easy-to-find way.**

✓ Find **one place where you can write all the important numbers you may need** (use a secret code if you are worried they might fall into the wrong hands).

✓ Use your **mobile and computer** to remind you of things that are important. I use my calendar and it makes a noise 5 minutes before I need to leave home and pick up the kids. It even reminds me to close the computer and tells me to "go home". (and I'm working from home)
.

✓ Think forward and **schedule backups** to important data, retrieving this information is painful.

✓ When you **need to focus**, turn off your mobile phone or put it on Silent. If it is hard for you, imagine yourself sitting on the toilet or taking a shower. You can always return the call later at a more convenient time.

✓ Keep an **up-to-date to-do list.** If you haven't finished something, move it to the following list so nothing gets lost.

✓ Prioritize your to-do list. Again, if it is in front of you, you can do it better than if you keep it in your head.

✓ Have a **time estimate** on each item of your to-do list. Over time, your time estimates will become more and more accurate.

✓ **Write a due date** on each of the items on your to-do list.

✓ **Write your own due date** on your to-do list. This item alone makes me much more effective. My magazine editor loves me, because she gives me the deadline, and I always have an earlier one of my own, taking into consideration other things I have to do. Many times, I give myself an extra month and I always send my articles in ahead of time. While she is running after other writers, I am always in her "good book".

✓ In your diary system, **schedule things that are similar together.** It can be things you can do in the same place, the same clothes, same state of mind. Some days I need to pick up Noff (my youngest daughter) at 3:00 and one of the older kids from the bus station at 4:00 and it is not worth coming home and then leaving again so I go to the supermarket next to my youngest daughter's school or the supermarket next to the bus station.

✓ When writing in your diary an appointment, make sure to **write the starting time and the end time**. It will make it easy for you to know how long the meeting will take and be more accurate scheduling something afterwards. If meetings require traveling time, include that as well in your starting and end time.

✓ Think of **things you could do while you drive**. I plan many things, practice for my presentations, do math with my daughter, plan our vacations, go over the family schedule and talk on the mobile with my clients and my sisters. I have a friend who spends a whole hour driving home from a client, so she records her findings on a digital recorder and gives it the next morning to her secretary to type into a report. She works all the way home.

✓ Find ways to shop **as fast as possible** – go to the supermarket when it is empty, on the way home, only shop with a list or order online. Since my sister had a baby, she started ordering online. For less than $3, she gets her groceries delivered and does not have to take her baby out and spend 2-3 hours shopping. She said it had been difficult for her to buy boxes of diapers, because her stroller is too small, and the supermarket is too far away from where she parks her car.

✓ Write 2-3 ideas to have an **efficient meeting**. Even meetings at home with your partner and kids can benefit from these ideas.

✓ **Be decisive.** If you start playing millions of scenarios in our head, you are trapped. Leave 3 options and choose one of them. It may not be the perfect one, but it is good to remember that not deciding what do to is a decision (not to do). If kids are stuck on it, give them 3 options and only examine them.

✓ Whatever you can delegate, **delegate!** Make sure to delegate to responsible people and follow up, so you won't have to do it twice.

✓ **Schedule time out** in your weekly plan.

✓ **Look at successful people.** Read biographies. Try to figure out how they manage their time.

✓ **It is good to be unique and creative, but it has a price.** When you are short of time, you are not unique and not creative. Sometimes it is better to go with the flow. Swimming against the stream is energy and time consuming. Being the first to do something can be very flattering but is very time consuming. **Let other people invest time in things you can just copy.**

✓ **Chunk sideways**. If you are stuck, think of a similar situation that you successfully handled. It does not have to be 100% the same but roughly the same for you to learn from your own experience. When helping kids chunk down, ask them, "What did you do last time something similar happened?" Remember, it is better to ask than to tell them what to do.

- ✓ **Perfectionism is a waste of time.** The main difference between good and perfect is how much more time you spend on things. It's not always worth it.

- ✓ Think of things you can do while you wait for your kids to finish their activities, at the dentist, at the bank, etc.

- ✓ **Wanting to be "right" is very time consuming and empties the confidence bowl.** You waste lots of time trying to convince others that your position/thought/action is the right one. Let go. There is more than one "right way" to do something and you picked the only one that you thought would benefit you. Justifying the past is not going to change the past. If you want more time in your life, stop trying to convince others that you are right and that your way is the "best" way. It is not! This item is a topic for a whole book. When you are trying to prove you are "right" you are flashing with your insecurities and that only empties your confidence "bucket" and takes a way plenty of precious time.

- ✓ Searching for the cheapest deal can be very time consuming. Driving two hours for a shop that sells a product for $2 less is not worth the petrol in your car nor your valuable time. **Weigh your time in your search for cheapness.**

- ✓ **Some people waste lots of energy on finding partners to achieve something.** It is true that in partnership you can achieve more but sometimes doing things alone saves lots of time and energy. Assess the trouble it takes you to find/convince someone to join you/believe in you/approve you and let go if it too time consuming.

- ✓ **Assess when team work can save you time and work on team skills.** One person cleaning the house takes much longer with lots of resentment than 4 people having fun.

- ✓ If you have difficulties making a decision, make a list of options and look at it when you are not sure. For example, if it is too hard for you to decide what to buy someone, make a list of ideas during the year. If deciding what to make for dinner is hard, have a list of ideas on the fridge and just look at that list when you need to.

- ✓ Time and effort equal results but when you **do things you are good at**, to get results you don't have to invest so much time and not much effort. Focus on things you do best and make them even better.

✓ Dreams are very important. Try not to live in dreamland all the time. **If you want something to happen, be active**. Ask yourself, what can I do now that will get me closer to my dream? And do it!

✓ **Do not over commit**. Whenever asked to do something, say, *"I need to check my calendar"*, *"I need to talk to my partner"* or *"let me get back to you"*. It'll give you the opportunity to check other commitments.

✓ **Doubts are huge inhibitors and are very time consuming**. Accept the fact you can't tell the future and that you are doing the best you can with what you have (skills, circumstances, abilities...). Small doubts are manageable, big doubts create anxiety. Use personal development to gain confidence. When working with your kids, do not doubt them very much as it will empty their confidence bowl.

✓ Check your routine. **Find out if a change in the routine can save you time**. I learned to marinate the meat straight after I buy it. When I take it from the freezer, it is already marinated so the routine of moving the meat from the freezer to the fridge in the morning saves me lots of time. When I start cooking in the evening the meat is already marinated and thawed.

✓ Have a **TV watching plan** to avoid one of the biggest time wasters.

✓ **Have a family calendar** (suggestions to come) to help kids follow up on everyone's timetable. If kids are too young, you can always have photos with magnets on the fridge that will help them understand the days of the week.

It takes 21 days to make a habit. If you find a tip that works, use it for 21 days until it is part of life (a habit) and then move on to the next item. That should give you more and more free time and set you free.

If you work on your list, I promise you will have over 100 things you can do. **Put this list where you can see** it and aim to implement every item on it and make them part of your life.

Time management quotes

I love quotes and I use them as great tips. I have collected many time management quotes for you to use. Read them and find those that seem like gems to you.

> Managing your time without setting priorities is like shooting randomly and calling whatever you hit the target.
>
> – Peter Turla

> Don't let the fear of the time it will take to accomplish something stand in the way of your doing it. The time will pass anyway; we might just as well put that passing time to the best possible use.
>
> – Earl Nightingale

> Time lost is never found again.
>
> – Benjamin Franklin

> Time is money.
>
> – Benjamin Franklin

> You delay, but time will not.
>
> -Benjamin Franklin

> Managing multiple projects is like being the parent of a large family that you have to feed. Each aspect of your job can be like another child that needs nurturing. You can't neglect any one of the 'children' and expect to have a healthy family.
>
> – Peter Turla

66 Everything requires time. It is the only truly universal condition. All work takes place in time and uses up time. Yet most people take for granted this unique, irreplaceable, and necessary resource. Nothing else, perhaps, distinguishes effective executives as much as their tender loving care of time.

— Peter F. Drucker

66 Time in its aging course teaches all things

— Aeschylus

66 Time is a file that wears and makes no noise

— English Proverb

66 "I recommend you take care of the minutes and the hours will take care of themselves.

-Earl of Chesterfield

66 It's better to do the right thing slowly than the wrong thing quickly.

— Peter Turla

66 He lives long that lives well; and time misspent is not lived but lost.

— Thomas Fuller

" Spare moments are the gold dust of time.

— Bishop Hail

" The ability to concentrate and to use your time well is everything if you want to succeed in business--or almost anywhere else for that matter.

— Lee Iacocca

" You will never find time for anything. If you want time, you must make it.

— Charles Buxton

" Take time: much may be gained by patience

— Latin Proverb

" The present moment is a powerful goddess.

— Johann Wolfgang von Goethe

" Those that make the best use of their time have none to spare.

— Thomas Fuller

" Be frugal of your time. It is one of the best jewels we have.

— Sir Matthew Hale

66   Time is a physician, which heals every grief

      – Diphilus

66   You can't change the past, but you can ruin the present by worrying about the future.

      – Unknown

66   Defer no time, delays have dangerous ends.

      – William Shakespeare

66   The common man is not concerned about the passage of time, the man of talent is driven by it.

      -Schopenhauer

66   Time is what we want most, but what we use worst.

      – William Penn

66   Time = life; therefore, waste your time and waste of your life, or master your time and master your life.

      – Alan Lakein

" Don't be fooled by the calendar. There are only as many days in the year as you make use of. One man gets only a week's value out of a year while another man gets a full year's value out of a week.

    – Charles Richards

" Ordinary people think merely of spending time. Great people think of using it.

    – Unknown

" Never let yesterday use up today.

    – Richard H. Nelson

" It's how we spend our time here and now, that really matters. If you are fed up with the way you have come to interact with time, change it.

    – Marcia Wieder

" Realize that now, in this moment of time, you are creating. You are creating your next moment. That is what's real.

    – Sara Paddison

" Time stays long enough for those who use it.

    – Leonardo Da Vinci

" All great achievements require time.

— Maya Angelou

" The time you enjoy wasting is not wasted time.

— Bertrand Russell

" All the forces in the world are not so powerful as an idea whose time has come.

— Victor Hugo

" The time for action is now. It's never too late to do something.

— Antoine de Saint-Exupery

" It is a mistake to look too far ahead. Only one link of the chain of destiny can be handled at a time.

— Winston Churchill

" The time to relax is when you don't have time for it.

— Sydney J. Harris

" Time stays, we go.

— H. L. Mencken

> The only reason for time is so that everything doesn't happen at once.
>
> – Albert Einstein

> Clock watchers never seem to be having a good time.
>
> – James Cash Penney

> Half our life is spent trying to find something to do with the time we have rushed through life trying to save.
>
> – Will Rogers

> There is nothing so useless as doing efficiently that which should not be done at all.
>
> – Peter F. Drucker

> Know the true value of time; snatch, seize, and enjoy every moment of it. No idleness, no laziness, no procrastination; Never put off till tomorrow what you can do today.
>
> – Lord Chesterfield

> Since time is the one immaterial object which we cannot influence — neither speed up nor slow down, add to nor diminish — it is an imponderably valuable gift.
>
> – Maya Angelou

" Work expands so as to fill the time available for its completion.

– Cyril Northcote Parkinson

" All the flowers of all of the tomorrows are in the seeds of today.

– Chinese Proverb

" You can't catch one hog when you're chasing two.

– Moe Schaffer

" Even if you're on the right track, you'll get run over if you just sit there.

– Will Rogers

" Take a rest. A field that has rested yields a beautiful crop.

– Roman poet Ovid

" The worst days of those who enjoy what they do are better than the best days of those who don't.

– Jim Rohn

" Don't spend a dollar's worth of time on a ten-cent decision.

– Peter Turla

❝ You must get good at one of two things. Planting in the spring or begging in the fall.

– Jim Rohn

❝ Half our life is spent trying to find something to do with the time we have rushed through life trying to save.

-Will Rogers

❝ Time is the school in which we learn, time is the fire in which we burn.

– Delmore Schwartz

❝ If you win the rat race, you're still a rat.

– Lily Tomlin

❝ Better three hours too soon then one minute too late

– William Shakespeare

❝ Time is the wisest counselor of all

– Pericles

❝ All that really belongs to us is time; even he who has nothing else has that.

– Baltasar Gracián

" Nothing is a waste of time if you use the experience wisely.

– Rodin

" Time as he grows old teaches many lessons.

– Aeschylus

" One thing you can't recycle is wasted time.

– Author Unknown

" Time is really the only capital that any human being has, and the only thing he can't afford to lose.

– Thomas Edison

" If you want to make good use of your time, you've got to know what's most important and then give it all you've got.

– Lee Iacocca

" You're writing the story of your life one moment at a time.

– Doc Childre and Howard Martin

" Lost wealth may be replaced by industry, lost knowledge by study, lost health by temperance or medicine, but lost time is gone forever.

– Samuel Smiles

66 The surest way to be late is to have plenty of time.

— Leo Kennedy

66 Your greatest resource is your time.

— Brian Tracy

66 A wise person does at once, what a fool does at last. Both do the same thing; only at different times.

— Baltasar Gracián

66 One worthwhile task carried to a successful conclusion is worth half-a-hundred half-finished tasks.

— Malcolm S. Forbes

66 To think too long about doing a thing often becomes its undoing.

— Eva Young

66 A year from now you will wish you had started today.

— Karen Lamb

> While we are postponing, life speeds by.
>
> — Seneca

> Don't say you don't have enough time. You have exactly the same number of hours per day that were given to Helen Keller, Pasteur, Michelangelo, Mother Teresa, Leonardo da Vinci, Thomas Jefferson, and Albert Einstein.
>
> — H. Jackson Brown

> Time is the coin of your life. It is the only coin you have, and only you can determine how it will be spent. Be careful lest you let other people spend it for you.
>
> — Carl Sandburg

> The great dividing line between success and failure can be expressed in five words: "I did not have time.
>
> — Franklin Field

> Live each day as if it be your last.
>
> — Marcus Aurelius, 140 AD

A stitch in time saves nine.

— popularized by Benjamin Franklin in his "Poor Richard's Almanac"

 There is a time in the life of every problem when it is big enough to see, yet small enough to solve.

— Mike Leavitt

Using a calendar

Encourage your kids to use a calendar. When they are young, buy them a themed calendar they like and teach them to use it every day. Here are some things kids can write in their calendars that will teach them planning.

Homework – tell your kids to write homework due dates. Teach them the importance of finishing their homework as soon as possible, when information is still fresh in their mind.

Assignments – tell your kids to write assignment due dates and plan backwards from them. Help them estimate how long it will take them to complete each assignment and teach them to always have a "time buffer", just in case they need some more time. I set "Ronit's due date" for assignments to a week before the official due date. This has saved me many times from not finishing assignments.

Special events (birthdays, parties, trips, family gatherings) – the kids can paste or staple invitations and permission slips to the right date and always be ready on time. (if they use a physical paper calendar)

To do list (bring jumping rope to school, return library book)

Time table for hobbies (basketball practice 3:30-4:30 on Mondays, music lesson 6:00-6:30 on Wednesdays)

Fun ideas for spare time (weekends are usually blank, so the kids can use them for general lists)

Phone numbers of friends – organized kids have names of friends with their phone numbers and preferably their parents' names and address. This is very useful when they plan a get together or some play time. It is also a good idea to have emergency numbers in the calendar and

Library days and due dates of library books

Focused action beats brilliance.

– Mark Sanborn

Start by doing what's necessary, then what's possible, and suddenly you are doing the impossible.

– St Francis of Assisi

Tips

✓   The most important thing about using a calendar is not having it but using it. If kids have a great calendar but never use it, it has no value. Every day, make sure you help your kids use their calendar. Go over their day and teach them to write down all the things they can think of and clear some space in their mind. Every day, make sure they look at the following day, week and month and plan what they need.

✓   The calendar can double up as a monitoring and confidence boosting tool by checking completed assignments and even writing down impressions and lessons learned which kids can look at again to remember.

✓   Keep doing this until you are confident your kids will use their calendar without your help

Deadlines

Using deadlines as a motivation tool can be a carrot or a stick depending on the style of the child. Some kids are last-minute kids – they are motivated to do things and get to their peak state when they have a tight deadline to meet. It excites and energizes them. Others dread deadlines and feel strangled by having a point in time by which they need to produce or do something.

If your child is a last-minute kid, although this is perceived a negative thing, it may bring out the best in them and yield the best outcome. So, if your kids study for exams only the night before and get an A – let them. If they do the project the day before its due date and get an A – let them.

For kids who perform badly under tight schedules, deadlines are a source of pressure. Encourage your kids to set their own deadline, as I explained above.

When kids set their own deadlines, they have a better feeling about controlling their time and they can take into consideration their other activities.

Family Calendar Tips

✓ Use a family calendar to be a role model and encourage family planning. A simple contact paper (sticky transparency) attached to your refrigerator or a centrally located door and some whiteboard markers will do the trick. Write down anything the family needs to take into consideration when planning something new.

✓ Encourage your kids to add their activities to the family calendar to give them a sense of belonging and to show their input is valued.

✓ Encourage your kids to ask "who, what, when and where". Once they get into the habit of asking these questions, they will be able to plan ahead better, because each question covers a different angle. For example, if they need to go to music lesson, they would ask *"Who will take me there?"* or *"How will I get there?"*, *"What do I need to take with me?"*, *"When does it start?"*, *"When should I practice?"* and *"Where are my notes?"*

✓ It is important to ask the right questions before we face the real challenge. Bear in mind that kids may not be able to think of every possibility initially, but they will get better with time, guidance and practice.

"Attitude is little thing that makes a big difference"
- Winston Churchill
© www.ronitbaras.com

Here are some examples of things you can help your kids plan and the questions they can ask:

1. **Plan a budget** – How much do I want to have? Until when? What for? How will I earn it? Who will help me? Where will I keep my money?

2. **Plan a party** – Who will I invite? When do I want the party to be? When should I send the invitations? How many kids can I invite? Where will the party be? What will be the theme of the party?

3. **Plan a trip** – Where do we want to go? For how long? When is the best time to go? What are we going to take with us? Who can we invite to join us? How much will it cost? What should we take with us?

4. **Plan a dinner menu** – How many people are coming? When are we going to sit down and eat? What do we need to buy ahead of time? What are we going to cook? Who will help? Where are we eating (dining room, balcony)?

5. **Plan for shopping** – What do we need to buy? When is the supermarket open? Who will go shopping? Where is the best place to buy meat/vegetables? How many loaves of bread do we need this week?

6. **Plan to fix something in the house** – What do we need to fix? Where is it? Where is the best place to start? How urgent it is? When is the best time to start? Who is going to help?

7. **Plan the weekend** – What do we want to do on the weekend? Who is already busy this weekend with other activities? Where can we go? When do we want to get up in the morning? How can we prepare ahead so we can get up later? What will the weather be like?

8. **Plan play time when hosting a friend** – Who am I going to invite to play? When? For how long? Where are we going to play? What are we going to play?

9. **Plan to go camping** – What do we need when it gets dark? Where is the flash light? How many meals? Who is coming? How many sleeping bags/plates/chairs do we need? How can we get everything into the car?

10. **Plan what to wear to school tomorrow** – What day of the week is tomorrow? What do I need to wear? Where can I put it? Who knows if my sports shirt is out of the laundry (no, it is not always Mom)?

11. **Plan what to do in case of fire at home** – How do I know there is fire? What do I need to pay attention to? Where do I need to go? Who do I need to call? How do I need to respond?

12. **Plan what to do when getting lost in the mall** – How can I tell I am lost? What do I do? Who (and how) should I call? Who is safe to approach for help? Where do I need to go?

13. **Plan what to do when in danger** – How do I know if I am in danger? What kinds of danger are there? Who do I need to stay away from? Who do I need to call for help (and how)? What can I do to stay safe? Where is it too dangerous to be?

14. **Plan what to do when talking to a stranger** – Who is a stranger? Who is not a stranger? Where (and when) is it safe to talk to people I do not know? What details should I never tell people I do not know? How can I keep myself safe from strangers?

15. **Plan to bake** – What do I want to bake? What do I need? Who is going to eat my cake/cookies? How long will it take? How long does it need to be in the oven? Where is the best place to put it in the oven? Who can help me? What is the first step? How to bake? When is it done?

16. **Plan to cook** – What do I want to cook? What do I need for cooking? Who is going to eat my food? How long will it take? Where is the best place on the stove to use? Who can help me? When is it done? What is the first step? Who is going to wash the dishes (tricky, this one)?

"If you think you can, you can. And if you think you can't, you're right"
- Mary Kay Ash
© www.ronitbaras.com

Summary

✓ Planning is a motivation technique that helps your kids **deal with their fear of the unknown**

✓ Planning is another form of **chunking down** and helps children (and their parents) with the overwhelming aspects of life. It gives them a sense of control over their lives and makes it much easier to be focused.

✓ **Master time management** if you want to raise kids who master time management. Collect tips and practice them. You can use time management quotes as inspiration.

✓ **Evaluate** your current time table, find your time wasters and seek ways to shrink them.

✓ **Use a calendar** to teach planning and have specific, detailed, huge to do lists.

✓ Use a **family calendar** to encourage collaboration and consideration between family members.

✓ **Deadlines can be a stick or a carrot**, depending on your kid's personal style. Follow the kids' style not yours.

✓ **Deadlines are only effective as self-motivators**. When people set their own deadlines and control their time table, they are more successful than those who have imposed deadlines.

✓ **Give your kids lots of practice time**. Children who practice time from an early age can master it and be very motivated based on their successful experiences.

✓ Use the what, where, when, who and how question to practice planning ahead.

13 CHAPTER THIRTEEN

TEAM WORK

For some kids, working together is a great motivator. Many times, when kids need to do something they do not know how to do, it is a big relief for them if someone else is experiencing the same challenges. Suddenly, they are not alone.

Teamwork helps when the fear of being lonely or the fear of shame and ridicule is strong. When kids are offered to work with other kids or even grownups, it will boost their confidence and allow them to take risks they would not take otherwise.

When I was a kid and my parents would give us cleaning tasks we hated, we would do anything to avoid doing the work. We would trade washing the dishes for endless favors and even for money. It was only when I was 16 years old that I found teamwork was a great motivator for me. My two younger sisters and I decided to share the burden of cleaning the house and after a while, it did not seem a chore anymore and turned into fun. Washing the house was faster, folding the laundry was faster and while we worked, we talked, joked and spent quality time together. Gradually, we also started cooking together and at night, when it was time to go to bed, it was hard for us to say good night and go to our own rooms. All my life I wanted to have my own room and during that time, having my own room wasn't an advantage at all.

"Things turn out best for the people who make the best of the way things turn out"
- *Art Linklette*
© www.ronitbaras.com

My children are very typical kids. They are very motivated by teamwork. Any work, however hard and however long, will be done to perfection when I offer to do it together with them.

The shared responsibility is a great help for such kids. When working in a team, they get permission to ask for help from other members of the team and ease the load of succeeding all by themselves. Such kids are very creative in a team and find ways to think out of the box that they could not find being by themselves.

Exercise: Are your kids team players?

To find out if your kids are motivated by teamwork, simply offer to do a task together with them and notice if the job is done faster and better.

Make sure it is not a suggestion to help but an offer to do it together. Help leaves the responsibility on the kids, while together means sharing the responsibility.

If your kids think your help is an excuse for them to run away from the job, this is not a good motivation technique for them.

Kids who are motivated by teamwork perform better academically when studying with another kid. If your kid does assignments better when a friend is around, they are motivated by teamwork. If working together with a friend makes them muck around, they are not the team player type.

Kids who are motivated by teamwork enjoy hobbies that require a group effort (hockey rather than chess, music ensembles rather than solo performance and so on).

Competition and motivation

For kids who like teamwork, a competition of teams can be a secondary motivator. However, when the competition becomes the focus rather than the teamwork, it destroys self-esteem and confidence instead of being a motivator.

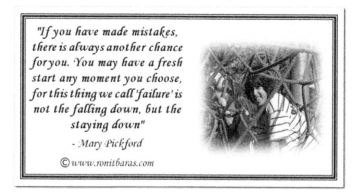

"If you have made mistakes, there is always another chance for you. You may have a fresh start any moment you choose, for this thing we call 'failure' is not the falling down, but the staying down"

- Mary Pickford

© www.ronitbaras.com

When using competitions as motivators, it is important to emphasize the fun, the sporting spirit, the teamwork and the relationships and not the end result. Overly competitive kids take any loss in a game or imperfection as failure and are unable to benefit from the teamwork. For example, if a kid is playing basketball and he is motivated by teamwork, he will pass the ball, follow the game plan and give other players a fair go in the game. If he is competitive, he will run to the basket, keep the ball to himself and will lose his temper and start blaming everyone around him when the score is unfavorable (*"The referee was against us"*, *"They were not fair"*), is this familiar?

Creating a motivating competition is a form of art. Every competition, when losing sight of the goal, becomes negative. On the other hand, every competition, when presented properly, works like magic.

Did you know?

Psychologists have tried to establish whether competition is natural and healthy aspect of humans. Sigmund Freud claimed humans are born competing for parents' attention and Charles Darwin claimed it is a survival instinct. Anthropologist Margaret Mead studied competition in societies and concluded it is a culturally created aspect of human behavior rather than natural behavior and is common in societies that highly value it.

Exercise: Are your kids too competitive?

Find out if your kids are motivated by competition in a positive way or too competitive to be on a team by paying attention to warning signs:

Do they make superior comments about others?

Do they blame others for their challenges, failures and difficulties?

Do they overuse word like "unfair", "wrong", "winning" and "losing"?

Many competitive kids are little mirrors of their parents. Pay attention to your behavior. Are you upset when your kids do not win or get first place? Do you express high expectations or disappointment towards your kids? If you do, the need to please you will create pressure on your kids to be competitive.

Make sure your competition is not perceived as war. To balance it, always remind your kids that teamwork is more important than winning.

Exercise

Motivating competitions

Make a list of competitions that will follow the rules of being motivators rather than war triggers. The basic idea is to set goals that are beneficial for everyone, no matter who "wins", and to put the emphasis on teamwork.

Here are some ideas you can choose from:

Competing with the clock – as boring as clearing the dinner table or getting organized for a trip may be, it can always be spiced up with *"Let's see how quickly we can finish this. I bet we can do it in…"It* is just an excuse to do our best, but we can pretend it is exciting while we are at it. My kids really go for this kind of thing, as long as everybody participates.

Kids vs. grownups – to prevent sibling rivalry, bring your kids together by competing with Mom and Dad. If you make sure you are not too competitive yourself, it might just work to your advantage. In that case, you are emphasizing group effort and teamwork instead of individual competition. For example, *"let's see if you can clear the table before I finish washing the dishes" "Let's see how long you can play together without me"*

Family race – if you have good friends with kids, you can encourage bonding within your family by having a family competition, like *"Who builds the best sand castle"*, *"Who puts up the tent first"* and a family treasure hunt.

Best supporting role – whether or not you give your kids an allowance, you can always give them rewards for helping out, being considerate or just being nice. Coupled with a competition for *"the biggest amount this week"*, your kids will be competing for being team players and winning even when they do not come first.

Teamwork as a motivator is generally easy to use with social kids but more needed for kids without social skills. Though there are some theories that supports genetic disposition to social skills there are many other behavioral theories that supports developing such skills. I believe that the combination of both is more accurate and while for some it will be easier to develop because of their natural talents and abilities, others, with the right guidance will be able to develop as well.

Summary

✓ **Teamwork can be a good source of motivation**. Performance should be better with kids that are motivated by teamwork.

✓ In team work kids can overcome their fears of being alone, shame and ridicule. They ask for more help and take more risks.

✓ **In a team, kids can overcome the burden of the responsibility with others**. It is important to teach them responsibility, but it needs to be developed slowly until they can carry it on their own.

✓ **Competition** can be a good motivator especially if it is in a team. Again, the shared responsibility is much easier to handle.

✓ **Bad competition** can be assessed when kids make superior comments, blame others for challenges and difficulties and talk lots about fairness, losing, winning.

- ✓ **Overly competitive kids** should not be encouraged to use this technique as a motivator. Every small failure destroys their self-esteem and empties their confidence bowl.

- ✓ To develop healthy competition, never lose the sight of the goal.

- ✓ If your kids are too competitive – **consider your attitude** – usually kids are mirrors. When you express lots of disappointment or high expectations or you are a bad competitor, your kids will copy you.

- ✓ Competition should emphasize the process and not the end result.

- ✓ Some **competitions that emphasize the team work**, like beating the clock, another team, helping together and kids vs. grownups are very **healthy and encourage**. When introducing competition place extra focus on teamwork.

- ✓ **Some kids naturally have better social skills** than others, but all kids need some ability to work with others. With the right guidance, everyone can improve on his/her team work skills.

PERMISSION TO MOTIVATE

Sometimes, the hardest thing for parents is to get their kids to accept their attempts to motivate them. Kids may treat parental attempts to motivate them as nagging or forcing when they have not given their permission to help them. Whether you like it or not, help is something that needs to be accepted.

I often say, "Parenting is not about what I give my kids, but about what my kids choose to take".

How can I help?

Before any attempt to motivate your kids, make sure this is something they want. Ask, "Would you like me to help you?", "What would you like me to do when I see that you're upset?" or "What do you suggest I do when you forget/come home late/fail Math?"

Many parents say they are not comfortable asking these questions because they are afraid the answer might be negative, but I think it is better to know than to pretend. Yes, there is a risk of your kid saying *"No, I don't want your help"*, but it gives you the option to leave the door open, in case they change their mind, by saying, *"Well, if you ever need me, I would love to help"*.

The **permission is a non-verbal contract** between you and your kids that allows you to take part in their life. It includes an acknowledgment that it is your kids' life and they will be the ones suffering or enjoying the consequences. It is an opportunity for you to make sure that motivating your kids does not create pressure on you and serves the kids' own definition of success.

"Parenting is not all about what I give, but about what my kids choose to take"

- Ronit Baras

© www.ronitbaras.com

Many parents fail to get their kids' permission to help. I hear parents say, *"But I only want what's best for him"* or *"But she is the most important thing to me"*. Yes, I know, most parents have lots of good intentions and lots of love, but intentions and love are not enough to convince your kids to do something. If you are a parent, you know what I mean.

In all my parenting workshops, parents ask me when supporting and helping their kids turns into nagging. The answer is simple. *"When you rate what is important to you higher than what is important to your child, you are nagging"*. Although your motivation techniques may be the same, the outcome will be totally different.

Supported and encouraged kids blossom while nagged kids misbehave, lie, hide and develop low self-esteem. Read this statement again and again. **Supported and encouraged kids blossom while nagged kids misbehave, lie, hide and develop low self-esteem**

 Exercise

Do you nag?

To understand the emotional reaction to nagging, try to find your interpretation to nagging by answering these questions:

Who nagged you as a kid?

Why did you consider this person a nagger?

What was that person's intention?

When this person nagged you, what did you want them to do instead?

What did this person nag about?

Who do you nag?

What do you nag about?

Why do you nag?

Tips

- ✓ Finding what nags you will help you understand your kids better. Everything you try, try on yourself first.

- ✓ Find more than one person who nagged you. This will help you find a pattern.

- ✓ Find a correlation between those who nagged you and the people you nag. It'll help you understand yourself and your kids

Fear of nagging

Kids who are nagged develop a fear of being nagged. Unfortunately, this fear makes them avoid getting into situations in which they might be nagged. They minimize their communication with their parents to avoid being nagged.

While mild nagging is a very common communication technique between parents and kids, nagging is a form of bullying. The nagger puts pressure (by saying something repeatedly, often in a whiny tone or with sarcasm) to do or not to do something and this creates an unpleasant experience for both sides.

Kids learn to nag from their surroundings. When they see nagging that works, they try it too. However, if their parents do not consider nagging a valid form of communication, the attempt will not be repeated.

Think of parents standing next to the cashier in the supermarket. Some parents are totally stressed while kids nag, and others aren't. Kids do not invent anything. If you nag, they will nag too. If you respect other people's desires, they will do that instead. As with anything else, nagging comes back like a boomerang and nagging parents raise nagging kids.

Remember: help without being asked may be considered an invasion.

What if they say "No"?

Whether kids welcome your offer to help and motivate them or not is an indication of how strong a relationship you have with them. If you have established a supportive relationship after getting permission, you may not need to ask again. In many homes, one parent has a relationship that permits this help and the other does not. Permission may be divided into topics. For example, Mom is good with math, so she can help with math and Dad is good with technical gadgets, so dad can help with that.

It is very important to understand that although your abilities and talents in a specific area attract your kids' requests for help, nagging overrides this very quickly. If your kids come for help and you nag, even if you are the best person in the world to help them, they will give it up.

Tips

✓ Kids say "No" when they are afraid that by giving permission, you will start nagging. Be specific about the area in which you would like to help and the type of help you are offering, and you may get a "Yes".

✓ Kids say "No" when getting your help means they are weak or inadequate. This may be because you are offering your help too soon and the kids want to try for themselves first. Be patient and you may be asked to help later.

✓ Kids say "No" when they think your offer is not sincere and you want to manipulate them. Take a hard look at the history of your offers and do your best to win back your kids' trust.

Check your relationship with your kids

When offering help to your kids or motivating them, it is important to examine yourself and your relationship with your kids and try to predict what their reaction will be. If you suspect they will reject your offer for help, find ways to gain their trust first.

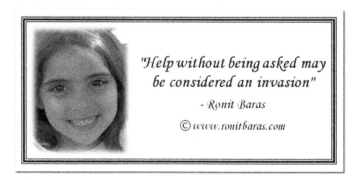

"Help without being asked may be considered an invasion"

- Ronit Baras

© www.ronitbaras.com

Exercise

Think of something you want to help your kids with and answer these questions:

Will he or she accept my help?

If so, what should I offer?

If not, why not? See the reasons your kid might refuse in the Tips box above.

What can I do to get a "Yes"? No, nagging is not a good idea…

Open door policy

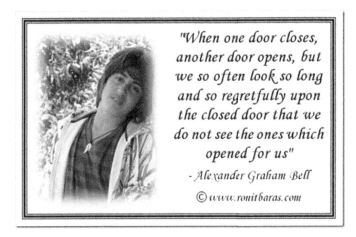

"When one door closes, another door opens, but we so often look so long and so regretfully upon the closed door that we do not see the ones which opened for us"

- Alexander Graham Bell

© www.ronitbaras.com

When kids choose to reject an offer, make sure they know they can come back any time. Sometimes, this is all kids need in order to feel motivated. They need to know they can rely on your help if needed. As teachers and therapist, we do our best never to "nag" the client and be very supportive even in very complicated situations, we say *"I am here, if you need me"*.

As a parent, never close doors. Always leave an opening for them to come. When you offer your help and your child says "No", not matter how hard it is, always say, *"I accept your choice and I want you to know that if you ever need help, I am here for you"*.

Kids sometimes regret having rejected an offer of help. Sometimes, they think about it later and realize they need it. Other times, they try, and find out they cannot do it by themselves or they realize they do not have enough experience to come up with the solutions themselves. Inside, all kids know Mom and Dad are the people who love them the most.

"Courage is never to let your actions
be influenced by your fears"
- Arthur Koestler

© www.ronitbaras.com

When your kids get to this understanding and come back, you need to be willing to help and motivate them to the best of your ability. If you are angry they said "no" and reacted badly to it, they will be very scared to come for help, even if they desperately need it.

I learned the open-door policy as part of my studies. When I started working with parents, I realized that most of them, feeling rejected, use threats, shame and guilt when their kids refuse to receive help. *"If you don't listen to me now, don't come back crying later"* or *"If you do that, you are not my child anymore"*. I have so many clients (too many, in fact) that have bad relationships with their own parents because they didn't pass this test. *"If you marry this guy, I don't want to have anything to do with you"* or *"I will help you study accounting but not art"*. Every family goes through that test. You pass the test if you handle your child's refusal to help with the open-door policy and fail it if you shut the door in anger.

Did you know?

Therapists use permission and the open-door policy in order to establish relationship with the kids they work with. They never put pressure on a kid to talk but rather create a safe space to allow exposure. Many kids will test the therapist by rejecting the offer to help several times before they trust the therapist by revealing information or emotions. If your child rejects your offer to help, remember to go into a test mode and keep the door open.

I once wrote a poem for my kids to make sure they fully understand the open-door policy. Print it and give it to your kids.

The Door is Always Open
- Ronit Baras

When you are happy, the door is open.
We are here to congratulate you on your success.

When you are sad, the door is open.
We are here to comfort you in your disappointment.

When you are lonely, the door is open.
We are here to keep you company.

When you are scared, the door is open.
We are here to spread our wings and shelter you.

When you feel you have failed, the door is open.
We are here to remind you of your great achievements.

When you are hungry, the door is open.
We are here to offer you the food on our table.

When you are in trouble, remember,
the door is always open.

When you feel lost, we are here.
Come. No need to knock.
We'll give you a compass to find your way

© *www.ronitbaras.com*

Summary

✓ **Permission** to help is necessary for the help to be effective and successful. It is not enough for you to want to help. Your kids need to want to receive help. It is a **non-verbal contract between the giver and receiver**. Intention and love are not enough!

✓ If parents try to motivate **without permission, kids may treat it as nagging or forcing**. It creates a fear of nagging and raises nagging kids that use avoidance as a coping mechanism.

✓ **Nagging many times is considered bullying.** It is a form of putting pressure on the listener by using words, sounds that judge, humiliate, ridicule and use sarcasm to force someone to do something.

✓ **Supported and encouraged kids blossom while nagged kids misbehave, lie, hide and develop low self-esteem.** Support becomes nagging when you rate what is important to you higher than what is important to your child. Nagging de-motivates kids.

✓ To understand the dynamic of nagging, **consider who nagged you and how do you nag, on what topics and why**? Find patterns and correlations between you and your own naggers. Try on yourself all strategies before experimenting on your kids.

✓ **Do not force your help: ask the child** "Do you need any help with that?" "Would you like me to help you?", "What would you like me to do when you are angry?" or "What do you suggest I do when you talk like this?" And take into consideration that it may be rejected.

✓ **Permission is a sign of good communication between kids and parents.** It keeps the motivation to succeed in your kids' hands. Nagging is a sign the relationship is missing respect. Nagging parents raise nagging kids. Nagging is an invasion or a boomerang.

✓ Your reaction to your kids' acceptance or refusal to get help will determine for many other times whether your child will come for help or not. **Kids will approve of help in some areas and others, not.** They **refuse your request for permission** when they are afraid of nagging, when they are worried to be considered weak, when there is lack of trust and they are afraid you will use this to manipulate them.

✓ No matter how hard it is to get a "no" to an offer to help, never shut the door in anger! **Always leave the door open** for them to come when they are ready.

GENTLE REMINDERS

When kids pursue their desires, whether they allow you to motivate them or not, they face difficulties and may be discouraged many times along the way. In fact, any unsuccessful event may cause them to give up. Their natural reaction may not be *"I should try something else"* but *"Maybe this is not important enough to me"*. After all, they are just kids, and this is a natural reaction for most people.

Giving up is a reaction to something that is seen as "too hard". Your job as a parent is to help your kids develop a "can do" attitude and not even consider the "other" option (giving up). Remember the parrot.

If you want to help your kids develop a "can do" attitude, you must be a "can do" person yourself. Role-modeling is always the best approach and it makes you an inspiring person for the little people around you. Being a role model is sending the message, without saying anything. It is also powerful because you do not ask your kids to do things you can't do yourself.

The second thing you can do to **remind** them **gently** what they want to achieve is to display and promote quotes that send the messages you wish to instill in your kids.

The great thing about the "Gentle Reminder" technique is that you can use it even when your kids have not given you permission to motivate them. This motivation is not as strong as some others, but it is as effective if done enough times. All you do is bring up the relevant topics, share your stories and allow your kids to soak them in.

Exercise – Be a role model

Answer these questions:

In which areas can you be an inspiration to your kids?

Where in your life have you achieved or overcome something with a "can do" attitude?

Have you told your kids about your successes?

"One may go a long way after one is tired"

- French Proverb

© www.ronitbaras.com

Tips

✓ Realize that some areas in life are easier for you to inspire them in.

✓ In areas where you are not a good model, find someone else to provide the encouragement. For example, divorced parents have a real challenge motivating their kids towards forming good long-term relationships, but may be able to turn to grandparents who have been together for ages.

✓ Find opportunities to tell your kids about what you have experienced, both good and bad, that brought you to where you are now.

✓ When you tell about yourself, do not ask for permission like, "Can I tell you about something that happened to me?" Instead, say, "This reminds me of…", "You know, when I was 6…" or "I want to tell you a story… "My own kids and all my clients love stories, so when I say I have a story, they are happy to listen. Sharing stories is a very gentle way to inspire people do things in general. Coaches, therapist, psychologists use it constantly and it is very successful.

To be honest, gentle reminders are another name for "mild nagging", but in a way, they are not invasive, and it is clear to all – parents and kids – that the child's agenda is being served.

It is very important to keep the reminders positive, otherwise the kids will do the opposite. Negative reminders reinforce the fact that the kids are not successful, incapable or not motivated and may involve a sarcastic spin. Sarcasm and negativity create fear and enlarge the gap between you and your kids, so stick to encouragement and support.

Did you know?

Thoughts, beliefs and values are stored in our brain as sentences that we adopt and **believe to be true.** They don't have to be true for us to adopt them and we carry them as rules for living. There are five major sources of thoughts, beliefs and values: our parents, education, life experience, media and our imagination and their strengths depend on the strength of the experience.

We easily adopt thoughts, beliefs and values if: we are young and have no filters, exposed to them by people who are close to us, when we are vulnerable and experience pain, and when we are exposed to them many times, or over a long period of time. If you want to instill good thoughts, beliefs and values in your kids' mind, evaluate your own thoughts, beliefs and values.

Tips

✓ Anything you want your kids to do, try on yourself first. It will help you learn what goes on in their heads.

✓ Avoid negative statements like *"You promised!"* Those trigger fear of disapproval, fear of failure, fear of criticism, guilt and shame.

✓ Avoid name calling. This will trigger the same fears including fear of rejection.

✓ Do not play the dark fortune teller – *"You will end up losing all your friends"", you won't have any money left"* or *"You will regret this".* Remember you are trying to help, not to force your kids to do what you think is best.

✓ Use questions – "Dan, when did you say you were going to start your project?" or "What are your plans for the project?" Questions are a wonderful way to overcome resistance.

✓ Sarcastic questions are not really questions. They are rude statements that mock the listener.

✓ You can offer help as a gentle reminder. Remind your kids you are there to help – "Alex, if you need my help with your spelling words, just tell me when", "I am here to help" or "Do you need any help with your project?"

✓ Remind your kids that the real reward is the final outcome and their own feeling of success and achievement.

✓ If your kids do not succeed, let them know it is not the end of the world. Nothing is the end of the world (except the end of the world, of course). Every pain is temporary and there is always something we can do to feel better. This will empower them to move forward.

✓ If your kids do not succeed, focus on how **they** feel (as opposed to how *you* feel). Ask them, *"How do you feel about it?"* or *"What do you think you can do next time?"* If they are very worried about what happened tell, say, *"There is no way for us to change what happened, but we can change what will happen in the future"*. Say it enough times and one day, your kids will start saying it to themselves.

Quotes are Great Gentle Reminders

One very gentle and effective way of reminding kids of all the things I have mentioned before is to introduce them to quotes. When someone else has said something, your kids may find it easier to accept. Think of the many things your parents have said to you that were harder to accept and how was it when someone else said the same thing.

Quotes are an easy way to instill a thought, a belief or an idea. All you have to do is post it in a place where your kids can read it. In our house, some doors are full of quotes, our fridge is covered with them and even in the toilet there are poems and quotes that we want our kids to adopt (while they sit there and ponder about the universe…). Most of the quotes we have, talk about character building, motivation, attitude, courage and self-esteem. By reading them over and over again, the thoughts become part of our being.

 Quotes are signs we put on our map to navigate through the journey called "life"

— Ronit Baras

I find quotes to be a very easy and successful inspiring tool in general. Quotes are signs we put on our map to navigate through the journey called "life". We need the signs to find our way through the happiness and sadness, joy and heartaches, challenges and successes. They are the guidelines for how we choose to live our life. When parenting, we need to make sure the guidelines are very clear and forward oriented.

My first quotes were sentences from songs I loved. When listening to songs, some people hear the melody. I always pay attention to the lyrics. Whenever I chose to carve them on my life map, I copied them into my diary and read them from time to time.

One song that was most meaningful for me as a teenager was John Lennon's "Imagine". On my year book, I wrote the quote *"You may say I'm a dreamer, but I'm not the only one. I hope someday you'll join us, and the world will be as one".* It is not a coincidence that today, many years later, I am the state director of Together for Humanity, a foundation advocating living in peace and harmony.

If you hear someone repeating a statement over and over again, you can tell lots about this person. It is the same for parents, whatever you repeat over and over again, your kids see as guidelines to navigate the world.

You can tell lots about people's personalities through their quotes. A person who repeats the quote *"Never, Never, Never give up!"*(Churchill) appreciates persistence. He/she may not be 100% persistent, but will definitely aim for it and appreciate it in others.

If a person says, *"Have faith in God. God has faith in you"* (Edwin Louise Cole), you can tell that this person is a person of faith.

If you want to instill something in your kids' mind, it is a good idea to find out the quotes that would motivate and inspire you to be the parents you want to be. The only thing to watch out for is funny quotes, because more often than not, they are sarcastic, and sarcasm is a form of emotional violence that no one wants their kids to adopt. If you have good quotes you can somehow contribute to your kids' thoughts, values, needs and beliefs and direct them towards a good life.

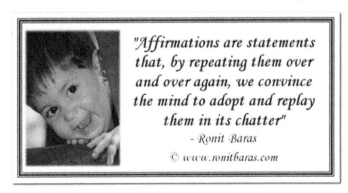

"Affirmations are statements that, by repeating them over and over again, we convince the mind to adopt and replay them in its chatter"
- Ronit Baras
© www.ronitbaras.com

Luckily, we can find a wealth of quotes on the Internet and they are all free. Here is a list of sites you can use to find good quotes and sayings you can instill in your kids and use them as gentle reminders to motivate them to do things they want. There are many sites and the list grows every day. I have chosen some to share with you.

- Quote Garden – I love this site and use it a lot.

- Quotations Page – The oldest quote site on the web.

- Wisdom Quotes – Another site I like using.

- Think Exist – More than 300,000 quotations by over 20,000 Authors.

- Quote Land – A bit overwhelming for a visual person like me, but still contains great quotes.

- Quotes and Sayings – Great site with quotes and saying.

- Brainy Quote – Easy to find by topic.

What we believe about our parenting has a direct impact on our family life. We manifest our beliefs to create the reality we believe we live in. I read many of the quotes I find over and over again, until they become part of me. Once they are part of me, when I repeat them over and over again to my children, they think it is coming from me.

Collecting quotes is a very practical tool for me as a person, an educator, a life coach and as I need all of those skills for my parenting, they are very useful even as a mother. To help you in this activity, I have collected many parents and parenting quotes I find very useful. I have written them in no particular order. You can go to any site or use this list as a starting point. These quotes are for you as a parent, some will be very useful to motivate your kids too.

I hope the quotes on this list inspire, motivate and encourage you on your parenting journey. Pick the ones you like and read them over and over until you feel they are a part of you.

" There are only two lasting bequests we can hope to give our children. One of these is roots, the other, wings

– Hodding Carter

" Parents need to fill a child's bucket of self-esteem so high that the rest of the world can't poke enough holes to drain it dry

– Alvin Price

" A mother understands what a child does not say

– Jewish Proverb

" Your children need your presence more than your presents

– Jesse Jackson

" The more people have studied different methods of bringing up children, the more they have come to the conclusion that what good mothers and fathers instinctively feel like doing for their babies is the best after all

– Benjamin Spock

" Father and child holding hands – If a child is to keep his inborn sense of wonder, he needs the companionship of at least one adult who can share it, rediscovering with him the joy, excitement and mystery of the world we live in

– Rachel Carson

" Never fear spoiling children by making them too happy. Happiness is the atmosphere in which all good affections grow

— Thomas Bray

" I talk and talk and talk, and I haven't taught people in 50 years what my father taught by example in one week

— Mario Cuomo

" There is always a moment in childhood when the door opens and lets the future in

— Graham Green

" The most important thing that parents can teach their children is how to get along without them

— Frank A. Clark

" All children behave as well as they are treated

— Anonymous

" Stop trying to perfect your child, but keep trying to perfect your relationship with him

— Dr. Henker

When You Thought I Wasn't Looking

When you thought I wasn't looking, I saw you hang up my first painting on the refrigerator, and I wanted to paint another one.

When you thought I wasn't looking, I saw you feed a stray cat, and I thought it was good to be kind to animals.

When you thought I wasn't looking, I saw you make my favorite cake for me, and I knew that little things are special things.

When you thought I wasn't looking, I heard you say a prayer, and I believed there is a God I could always talk to.

When you thought I wasn't looking, I felt you kiss me goodnight, and I felt loved.

When you thought I wasn't looking, I saw that you cared, and I wanted to be everything that I could be.

When you thought I wasn't looking, I LOOKED... and wanted to say thanks for all the things I saw when you thought I wasn't looking.

– Unknown

Life affords no greater responsibility, no greater privilege, than the raising of the next generation

– C. Everett Koop

Praise your children openly, reprehend them secretly

– W. Cecil

To be in your children's memories tomorrow, you have to be in their lives today

– Anonymous

Children Learn What They Live

If a child lives with criticism, he learns to condemn.

If a child lives with hostility, he learns to fight.

If a child lives with ridicule, he learns to be shy.

If a child learns to feel shame, he learns to feel guilty.

If a child lives with tolerance, he learns to be patient.

If a child lives with encouragement, he learns confidence.

If a child lives with praise, he learns to appreciate.

If a child lives with fairness, he learns justice.

If a child lives with security, he learns to have faith.

If a child lives with approval, he learns to like himself.

If a child lives with acceptance and friendship, he learns to find love in the world.

– Dorothy Law Neite

The most important thing a father can do for his children is to love their mother, and the most important thing a mother can do for her children is to love their father

– Anonymous

> A father is someone who carries pictures where his money used to be
>
> — Lion

> Of all the rights of women, the greatest is to be a mother
>
> — Lin Yutang

> A baby will make love stronger, days shorter, nights longer, bankroll smaller, home happier, clothes shabbier, the past forgotten, and the future worth living for
>
> — Anonymous

> God could not be everywhere, and therefore he created mothers
>
> — Jewish proverb

> The child of a tiger is a tiger
>
> — Haitian proverb

And my final one:

> Creativity, flexibility, tolerance and love are natural states of mind and our purpose is to nurture them to full blossom
>
> — Ronit Baras (from the book "Be Special, Be Yourself for Teenagers")

Again, remember that when you get into the habit of collecting quotes, your kids can learn lots about you.

Tips for collecting quotes for yourself

✓ Remember, quotes do not need to be written by famous people to be good. Something your grandpa used to say can be a great quote to live by too. Think of things people close to you repeatedly said, if you believe in it, it is a quote worth adding to your collection.

✓ If you find that you like several quotes by the same author, you probably share something with this author. Check out other quotes by this person. Can you tell I like Buddha's quotes?

✓ Songs are great sources of quotes. If you love the lyrics of a song, quote them. I love Jewel's "Hands", in which she sings, "If I could tell the world just one thing, it would be that we're all OK" and "Only kindness matters". I repeat the words and listen to the song so many times and it helps me tell my kids that "everything will be OK" and that I value kindness.

✓ The library is full of books with quotes. If you prefer to hold a book and find quotes in it, go to the library.

✓ When reading books with quotes you like, copy them in your diary, computer.

✓ Display your quotes in a visible place. You can put them on the shower, toilet, fridge, the entrance to the house… (I have a very famous toilet with so many quotes that everyone who enters my quote temple is very happy to spend his time reading them)

✓ It is very natural that we change our quotes as the circumstances of our life changes. A young person adds quotes about fun and adventures, but as they grow, they add quotes about family and stability. Change is only a sign of evolution and maturity. There is no right or wrong, only what is suitable for you **now**.

✓ Stay away from depressing quotes that bring doubt and anger and from quotes that trigger fear.

✓ Stay away from sarcastic quotes. As I said before, their undertone is not funny at all. Sarcasm is an expression of frustration and not hope.

✓ Stay away from stereotypical quotes about gender, race, nationality, sexual preferences, etc. They may be funny, but your smile may disappear when you end up believing in them.

I have a history of inspiring other with my quotes. When my young sister travelled to India and Thailand for six months, I bought her a journal and on every other page, I wrote a quote about travelling, about being safe and confident and about self-discovery. She said that every time she wrote in her journal, the quotes I had written were the most appropriate for the emotional growth she was experiencing.

My students used to say to each other the things I have been repeating over and over again and recently, I spent a month with my nephew and niece who are just 4 years old and 2 years old and a week after I left, they started repeating my sentences.

Some of my clients, who are aware of each other (They referred each other to me) quote me in their conversations. Sometimes when they come for a session after a very long break and tell me about their adventures they say. *"I asked myself what would Ronit say and I knew immediately what to do"*. I have sentences I repeatedly say, and they can easily use them as a guide when they are confused and need to make decisions.

As you have already seen throughout the book, I have added many quotes and poems to motivate kids. I encourage you to print the ones you like the most and post them in places where you and your kids can see them often.

Tips for collecting quotes to motivate your kids

✓ Collect quotes that mean something to you. As I said, there are many quote sites on the Internet and many thousands of quotes in each of them, so search for any topic with the word "quotes"" parenting" "motivation" to find them

✓ Make sure the quotes are suitable for your kids' ages – consider the topic and level of language to ensure the message is clear. For younger kids, do not use fancy words they may not understand. It will dilute your message.

✓ If the quotes are in your head, it is best to get them out of there and display them where your kids can see them

✓ Make sure your quotes are positive and not negative (*"Love thy neighbor"*, not *"Don't hate thy neighbor"*). I love the quote *"Never, never, never give up"* but it is a negative quote. What a shame!

✓ Stay away from sarcastic quotes – they may be funny on the surface, but their underlying message is about being powerless, helpless and hopeless. Remember, quotes supposed to give kids courage, hope, confidence, trust and happiness.

✓ Come up with your own quotes. If you say something to your kids repeatedly, make it a quote. I have a quote that is only mine and my kids know this quote by heart – *"My mommy loves me a million million"*. I have said it to my kids so many times by now that if you come in the middle of the night and whisper *"My mommy"* in their ears, they will automatically mumble *"loves me a million million"*. I even sign notes, emails and text messages to them with *"million million"*.

✓ Make your quotes look attractive to draw your kids' attention to them – use colored paper or lots of color, special fonts, bold print, images and stickers, make them big, 3-dimensional or laminated. Remember, if they see it over and over again, their brain records them over and over again until it becomes a thought.

✓ By posting your quotes around the house, you can guarantee your kids will be exposed to them even when you are not physically next to them. Entrances, albums, showers, mirrors, doors, toilets and diaries are only some of the place where you can post your quotes.

Quotes are fantastic gentle reminders. They help you pass on a message without saying anything. They are a form of modeling, because you share them with your children, and you only share things you believe in.

After all, parents are salespeople, selling their philosophy on life to their kids. The only way to check if your kids have "bought" your philosophy is to wait and see if they use it with their own children. Until then, you must work on your "product" and make sure it delivers value.

Quotes become part of your "product", your parenting and life philosophy. If you display them, use them and repeat them, they will become part of your kids' "parrot" and will help their decision-making process in the future.

It is good to remember that with those "reminders", you are helping your children achieve something **they** want and gain control over their life. They are considered gentle especially by teens, who resist parental help.

Summary

✓ Giving up is a natural reaction to inability to handle disappointment or failure. A Can-do attitude is a good way to make sure your motivation tools will be sustainable.

✓ "Can do" parents raise "can do" kids. It is easy. Just be a role model.

✓ Find the things you can inspire your kids to do. Inspiration is a very gentle and effective motivating strategy. If you can't be an inspiration, find someone who can.

- ✓ Share your own inspiration and learning experiences to use them as motivation. Don't ask permission! Don't use sarcasm or negative statements, don't use name calling and don't be a dark prophet. It triggers fear.

- ✓ Use questions as reminders. If they are not sarcastic, they will be just reminders.

- ✓ Offer to help as a gentle reminder.

- ✓ Make sure you are not too focused on what you feel but what your kids feel. It is better to keep the motivation where it needs to be – in your kids' hands – and the topic here is what they want and feel.

- ✓ Quotes are excellent gentle reminders and function as guidelines. When we repeat them over and over again, they become a belief. It is true when we say good things and unfortunately true when we say bad things about ourselves and others. If you say over and over again to your kids "you are lazy", eventually, they will believe they are lazy. It will be harder to get rid of this self-belief than to get rid of their so called "laziness". If you tell your kids, "you are so creative", eventually, they will believe they are creative, and it will be as hard to get rid of that thought as well. (But who wants to get rid of this thought anyway!)

- ✓ You can find quotes in sentences you use, people you know, movies, books and quote sites. There are millions of them. You can have a family quote book if you wish. They are free to use.

- ✓ Sometimes hearing it from someone else does the trick. It is a very gentle way of saying "It is not me who is saying it" and kids are more accepting if it is from other sources. The other person doesn't have to be hot and famous; it can be a grandparent, your boss, someone you know. Be honest, share the source and never make it up. Young kids don't know who Buddha was, but his quotes are still very effective.

- ✓ Kids can learn a lot about you from the quotes you use. Find inspiring quotes you can adopt as a parent that by following them you become a living example of the ideas you wish your kids to have.

✓ Pick quotes that have the message you wish to promote. Match them to age, language level and stick to positive and clear messages. Stay away from sarcastic quotes (no, your kid's subconscious won't think they are funny. The Subconscious does not have a good sense of humor). Print them, make them attractive and post them in a visible place.

AFFIRMATION FOR SELF MOTIVATION

Affirmations are a good way to encourage your kids to move forward. They are the quotes you have engraved in your kid's mind that will guide them in life. Instead of telling them you do not want them to give up, you give them an affirmation that tells them not to give up. The great thing about affirmations is that they are self-motivating, and they never end. Once they are planted in the mind and the person possessing them benefit from them, he/she will keep using them to navigate through life forever.

If you want to instill good affirmations in your kids' mind so they can use it to motivate themselves, it is a good idea to understand the science of affirmations.

Affirmations are statements that, by repeating them over and over again, we convince the mind to adopt and replay them in its chatter

- Ronit Baras

"Hello me, this is Ronit"

Whether we speak out loud or we are in silence, our brain is in continuous chatter. We have thoughts about things to do, feelings, expectations, ideas, reminders, theories and conversations. Here is an example of my mind chatter in the first 10 seconds in the morning. I still had my eyes closed and said nothing at all:

"What's that noise? ... What's the time? ... 6:30 ... Oh, no, Noff has swimming today ... I wanted to put a bottle in the freezer for her ... I forgot ... It's going to be hot today ... I should have gone to bed early last night ... I talked to my sister ... I miss her ... Two more seconds ... I have to get up now ... I'll go to sleep early tonight ... Yes, I said that yesterday too ... I'll meditate ... "

Everyone's brain is full of such talk and the difference between people is the kind of thoughts they have or rather the direction of their thoughts.

A very simple way of categorizing thoughts is to divide them into positive and negative thoughts. Positive ones are full of hope or love and negative ones are full of fear or frustration. Hope will increase the flow of good chemicals in the body and promote health, while fear will increase the flow of bad chemicals that will promote sickness. It is as simple as that!

Affirmations are thoughts that repeat. They get into our chatter constantly and are in the same form. Much like a thought, some affirmations are positive and will motivate us to be and do great, courageous, happy, successful things and others are negative and they will prevent us from doing, being, trying things. Here are simple examples.

"I can do it!" is a very healthy affirmation.

"I can't do it!" is a very negative and debilitating affirmation

And you, the parent can decide which one of those affirmations will be carved on your kids' mind and be repeated by their parrot. All you need is a bit of understanding of the way our brain functions.

A tour guide for the brain

The mind chatter works as a guide to our attitude and behavior. Think of a tour guide sitting in your head and directing your actions to happiness, health, success and achievements or to sadness, sickness, disappointment and failure.

Here is a simple example of how mind chatter can affect someone. Bryan is on his way to a job interview. He is driving his car to the city, where he is supposed to meet the manager and two members of the team he wants to join. The recruitment agent has said there were 5 people applying for the job.

This is Bryan, with lots of positive affirmations, driving his car to the job interview:

"I can do it ... I will talk about the project I did last year ... I am very good with people ... Deep breath ... It'll be fine ... I'll learn from it anyway ... I need to stay focused ... Five people ... That's not many ... I have lots of experience ... It's a good job ... I really want it ... I'll do my best"

And this is Bryan, with negative affirmations, on his way to the same job interview:

"I hate interviews ... I don't know what to talk about ... I am not so good with people ... I can't breathe ... It'll be a shocker ... What if they ask me about my previous boss? ... Five others against me ... I don't have a chance ... The young candidates always have an advantage ... It's going to be too hard ... Why do they have to bring three people for the interview? ... It'll be another disaster"

You can easily predict how the positive Bryan will handle the interview and how the negative Bryan will handle it even before they step into the interview room. In the same way, you can predict Bryan's relationships, finances and state of health. If Bryan was your child, you would be able to predict his success in everything he does in life.

Our kids are "Bryans" and we can make sure their chatter box/Max the parrot say the positive motivating things the second they face a difficultly.

Much of our mind chatter is thoughts we have been given by others, thoughts based on past experiences we have had (as kids), things we have seen in the media and interpretations of what has happened around us. This is the reason we say that our parents, or the people close to us, like family and close teachers, are the main contributors to this chatter box. It is much easier to instill a new thought than to replace a damaging one, this is why the earlier you start, the easier it is the plant the seeds in your kids' mind.

One day, when I explained to my daughter the concept of the good and healthy affirmations and the non-healthy one, she drew a picture for me that was brilliant (who says you can't learn from your own kids, she was only 14 back then). Think of an affirmation as a seed. It can be a seed that grows flowers, which will become nutritious fruits or seeds that grow dark and poisonous fruits. Things you are saying will become seeds, you have the power to determine if they will grow sweet fruits or poisonous ones. Parents are the gardeners and with their words and actions, they plant seeds and water them.

Bear in mind, it is never too late to uproot a rotten affirmation plant, with nutritious affirmations but it is harder if the tree has been there in the mind for a long time, has been watered and has grown branches. It is harder, but not impossible. Whenever you consider critical time, I want you to know that NOW, is always better than LATER. When we talk about kids, as long as you call them your kids, even if they are 50 years old, your words and actions are critical and has the potential to water good affirmations seeds and uproot (or at least not water) the poisonous affirmation seeds.

As parents, we want to motivate our kids and can't stop thinking of the time when they will have to be able to do it to themselves, even if we won't be there. Here is a story I wrote that describes every parent's dream.

10 mothers sat in a coffee shop and talked about all the things they wanted for their kids.

The first mother said, "I wish I could give my kids lots of money so they could have everything they want and be financially free".

The second mother said, "I wish I could give my kids knowledge to help them succeed in life. Learning is the way to growth and knowledge is the key to success."

The third mother said, "I wish I could give my kids wonderful friends to keep them company for the rest of their lives".

The fourth mother said, "I wish I could give my kids strength to overcome all the difficulties in life".

The fifth mother said, "I wish I could give my kids compassion and kindness towards themselves and towards others, for compassion and kindness bring all people together and make us one".

The sixth mother said, "I wish I could give my kids acceptance to help them flow with the stream of life and lead them to spirituality".

> The seventh mother said, "I wish that I could give my kids gratitude for all that the universe has to offer them, for gratitude is the vibration of all good things in life".
>
> The eighth mother said, "I wish I could give my kids perfect health so they can experience the world with all their senses".
>
> The ninth mother said, "I wish I could give my kids love. Love is everything and love is the answer to all".
>
> The tenth mother said, "I want to give my kids happy thoughts that can lead them to financial freedom, knowledge, friendship, strength, compassion and kindness. A happy, positive mindset will lead them to acceptance, gratitude, health and love, for happiness is the ultimate state of bliss and happy thoughts are the way to get there".

As a parent, you can instill good affirmations in **two ways: by saying things or modeling them**. For both, you need **consistency in modeling** and **repetition in your words** and they **must be in sync**. You can't plant the *"your health is very important"* when you smoke and eat junk. Remember, your actions speak louder than words.

Consistency and repetition will guarantee the plant will never be dry or be too wet. It is like adjusting the water to water the plant in specific times and in just the right quantity.

To make sure you are consistent and model well, it is good to monitor the affirmations you have as a parent. As much as it is hard to admit, your kids will adopt them regardless of their effectiveness. Some of them you may have to change (if you don't want your kids to have them as well) and some you would want to instill in your kids' mind.

 Exercise: Affirmation stock take

Your mission (should you choose to accept) is to collect a list of beliefs/thoughts/affirmations you have in many areas of life. It will help you be more conscious about the things you repeatedly say and do to your kids and determine whether you are planting seeds of confidence or poisonous fear. Once you find the beliefs/affirmations assess whether they are good to have, which of them you would like to change and which of them you would like to instill in your children. Good ones instill hope and courage, bad ones create fear.

Tips for making a list and using it

✓ Try to reach 100 beliefs. If you are worried you won't find that many, remember that every thought you have in your mind that you believe it to be true is a form of affirmation. You have millions of them. This activity only brings them to the surface.

✓ Ask yourself *"When I die, what would my kids say about me?"* if answering it scares you, it is a sign you need to make some changes. If you are happy with the thought, check if you dedicate much time to support this thought.

✓ If you feel overwhelmed a bit and have no idea of what to write, here is a list of topics you have some thoughts about: kids, parenting, home, relationships, family, success, school, knowledge, love, friendship, money, health, work, social issues, studying, high education, philosophy , gender, history, technology, personal development, feelings, medicine, hobbies, time, spirituality... I recommend you write 5-10 things you think about each topic and you'll get to 100 easily.

✓ Quotes you like are good places to search for the affirmations you have. If you quote something/someone over and over again, it means your brain believes it is true.

✓ Write down your affirmations. Writing will help you fight the mind chatter. Do not be tempted to say, *"I will remember"*. There is nothing to remember. You are trying to find out what kind of maps your crew is using to navigate your life. Your crew will not give them to you easily. If writing is not your thing, record yourself saying it and listen to it often.

✓ Once you find good beliefs, use "I" statements. To convince your mind to accept any thought, you have to take full responsibility for it. Statements about other people can help as well (*"People are friendly to me"*, *"Everyone appreciates me"*), but the focus is wrong because you use the approval trap as motivation and external approval is not a healthy motivator. Use short, simple statements. Though we even have affirmations in a form of a" story" (this is why in coaching or any form of therapy, we refer to the stories of our lives) it is much eas*ier to repeat a short simple statement. Yes, when you w*ant to instill it in your kids' mind, you can share the story, but the story is not the important thing, the conclusion is.

✓ Try focusing on positive affirmations in present tense. *"I am happy"* instead of *"I will be happy tomorrow"* or it will highlight that you are not happy now.

✓ Avoid conditions in your statements like *"I will be happy when..."* The conditions you place on feeling good tells kids that you will not settle for any happiness and it will make it harder for you to feel happy.

✓ If you can, change negative statements to positive ones. It helps with motivation. Say, *"I feel healthy and fit"*, instead of *"I am not sick anymore"*. Say, *"I accept others"*, instead of *"I do not criticize others"*. Say, *"I had a good day"*, rather than *"Not bad"*.

✓ To assess your affirmation, watch the language of the people you hang round with. When they say, "Tell me who your friends are, and I'll tell you who you are" they mean that you reflect your friends' belief system. So, hang around people with positive thoughts and affirmations and encourage your kids to do the same. Stay away from complainers, victims, aggressive, frustrated or critical people. If you are the complainer, victim, aggressive, frustrated and critical person, you need to take time out from yourself and make a mind overhaul. (A life coach can help you do that).

Once you are aware of your own affirmations, you can use your successful ones and plant them as a guide in your kids mind so they will be able to motivate themselves even long after they do not live in your house with your support, to rise up and succeed in whatever they wish to do.

I believe that self-esteem is the fuel for self-motivation and parenting is the art of building our kids' self-esteem so they can keep going forward towards all their desires in life.

In a way, motivating your kids is like giving them a fish, while teaching them to motivate themselves is like giving them the fishing net.

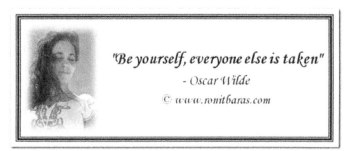

"*Be yourself, everyone else is taken*"
- Oscar Wilde
© www.ronitbaras.com

Self-motivating affirmation ideas

Here is a list of "fishing nets" that would work very well and make sure your kids have a supply of "fish" that will last them a life time. I have accumulated a list of thoughts that successfully motivate kids to move forward. Some statements are different versions of the same idea. Some are self-explanatory or have been covered before. Make sure you examine all the quotes here to help you pick those you wish to implant in your kids' mind. In time, together, they will become a toolkit they can use to motivate themselves. Some thoughts come with some tips to instill them in kids. Many of the tips are suitable for different thoughts. Pick the ones most suitable to you.

 **Exercise**

You can, if you are brave enough, give your kids the list of thoughts (without the suggestions to instill them) and ask them, "*Do you think you have this thought in you?*" and after you will know what they already have and what is still missing, ask, "*Which of them would you like to have? And what do you think I can do to help you adopt it?*"

This whole book is full of ideas on how to motivate your kids. If they express a desire to adopt some of the affirmations in this list, practice the toolkit in this book to help them achieve it.

✄ "**I treat others the way I want them to treat me.** If I want people to help me, I help others. If I want them to encourage me, I encourage others. If I want them to love me, I love others"

✖ "I know there are many ways to do one thing. **I accept that not all people think the same and that not everyone thinks like me.** My way is best for me. It is OK for people to think differently"

✖ "**Many hands make light work".** When I share, help or cooperate with others, I can achieve more"

✖ "When I am angry, I control myself and **never hurt myself or others"**

✖ "I am **honest** and **say what is on my mind in a nice way without hurting others"**

✖ "When I am in trouble, I can **ask for help**. Many people around me can help me"

Tips for teaching kids to ask for help

1. Talk to your kids about help. What is help?

2. Emphasize working together and teamwork

3. Use statements of sharing and caring. Parents using "we" as a motivating tool are better leaders.

4. Talk about your own need for help to teach that help is not a weakness

5. Volunteer with your kids to do acts of kindness and talk to your kids about the emotional reward

6. Talk about the importance of taking care of ourselves

7. Talk about assertiveness and teach ways to express needs without getting into a conflict

8. Talk about acceptance

✖ "**When I am sad, I can do something that makes me happy.** I have hundreds of things that can make me happy and I do not need others to give them to me. I can give them to myself"

Tips to help kids manage their feelings

1. Make sure your kids have a **happy list**. It is a list of things that can make them happy. Not necessarily things you buy them but simple things that changes their mood instantly like, inviting friends over.

2. Help your kids plan what to do when they are sad. In our house, we eat, sleep, meditate and choose something from our happy list…

3. Tell your kids that happiness is a choice. It is a good slogan to empower kids and make sure they will not adopt a victim mentality.

"Fear and courage are brothers"
- Proverb
© www.ronitbaras.com

✂ **"When I play, I follow the rules and play fair.** I take turns and I understand that winning means nothing if it means losing a friend"

Tips for helping kids play fair

1. Playing by the rules is a way to avoid frustration. In every game, there are winners and there are losers, but the game is fun as long as it stays a game. Discuss "sore losers" and why they don't have friends at all.

2. Pay attention to your reaction when your kids lose. Most kids learn to be sore losers from their own parents.

3. Emphasize teamwork and friendship

4. Focus on what we gain from playing and participating and the process rather than the outcome.

✂ "Gossip is not productive. **I avoid gossip.** If I talk about someone behind his or her back, I always say something positive"

Tips for encouraging kids to avoid gossip

1. Be positive when you talk about other people in front of your kids. They hear everything you say about the in-laws, your boss, your wife and husband. We have a rule that says if you have something good to say, say it! If not, keep it to yourself. There is always something good to say about others, if you can't, it does not mean there is nothing good to say, it only means you haven't found it, yet! Keep looking.

2. Whenever you talk about someone else, make sure to divert the conversation towards "good things". When your kids are upset or angry at someone, say, *"I understand you are not happy about what he/she did, but…"* and add something positive, like, *"He/she is still a good friend"*, *"We all make mistakes sometimes"* or *"You still like playing with him/her"*

3. If you have something not nice to say about someone, always say it to the person you have the issue with and not to a third person. There is a simple rule that says, if you can say it to the person to their face, it is not a gossip.

✖ **"I treat everyone with respect.** I respect other people's opinions, even when they do not think like me"

Tips for teaching kids respect

1. The best way to teach respect is to be respectful parents. Ask your kids for their opinion about your own behavior. Remember, it is not a competition or a "balancing the compliments" act but it is to show them they are valued.

2. When you disagree, say, *"I disagree"* or *"I think differently"*. Never downplay your kids' opinion and especially not in front of others.

3. When you disagree with your friends about things, be honest. Show your kids you don't agree with your friends about everything, but you are still their friend

✖ **"I spend my time with successful kids** and learn a lot from them"

Tips for associating your kids with successful kids

1. Pick out kids you would like your kids to hang out with and tell your kids why you would like them to associate with those kids

2. Get to know those kids' parents

3. Encourage your kids to invite those friends to play

4. A great party can seriously boost a kid's popularity among their friends. Throw a party for your kids at least once a year

5. When your kids are invited to parties and events with other kids, go along and socialize with the other parents

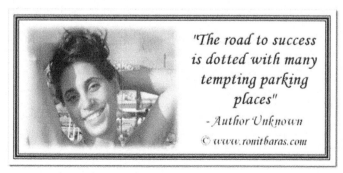

"The road to success is dotted with many tempting parking places"

- Author Unknown

© www.ronitbaras.com

- "I am not the way I look. **My look is just external**. When I feel good, I look good, so I dedicate my time to feeling good"

Tips for supporting kids' self-image

1. Kids' bother a lot with the way they look. Tell them they look great! You can always find something nice to say – their smile, their hair, the way they hold their head, their eyelashes…
2. Talk to your kids about successful people who do not look like everyone else (they may be fat or short, they may wear glasses, etc.) to separate success from looks.
3. Talk to your kids about the difference between magazine photos and reality. Explain what photo shop is and develop their critical thinking
4. Encourage your kids to take care of their body but link it to health.

- "I **appreciate my family** for all that they have done and still do for me"

Tips for encouraging family appreciation

1. Talk to your kids about the value of family.
2. Express your appreciation for what your family is doing for you. Focus on what you have in the family rather than what is missing.
3. Let your kids watch movies about family values.
4. Spend time with families that share the same values that you would like to encourage.
5. Work on your relationship with your own parents and siblings to be a role model for family values.

- "**I can do anything I put my mind to**"

Tips for raising "can do" kids

1. Bring movies and books about people winning against all odds.
2. Tell your kids stories about you succeeding against all odds.

- "**I can make a difference in this world**"

Tips for empowering kids to make a difference

1. Teach your kids how simple things (like turning off the tap or the light) can make a difference in the world.

2. Donate to charity.

3. Donate your time and show them that the real reward of giving is a wonderful feeling of being kind.

- "I know how to listen. **When I listen, I show others that I care**"

Tips for teaching kids to be good listeners

1. Start by listening to your kids.

2. Teach your kids to count to 10 before saying things in anger.

3. Have family meetings at dinnertime and encourage everyone to listen to each other.

- "Friends are attracted to kindness. **When I am kind, I have kind friends"**

- **"Sharing with others makes me feel good** and makes them feel good too"

- "**When I help others, I feel good"**

- "**I am a supportive friend**. I encourage my friends to do their best"

- "Others decide if they like me by what I say and how I say it. **I am mindful of what I say and how I say it"**

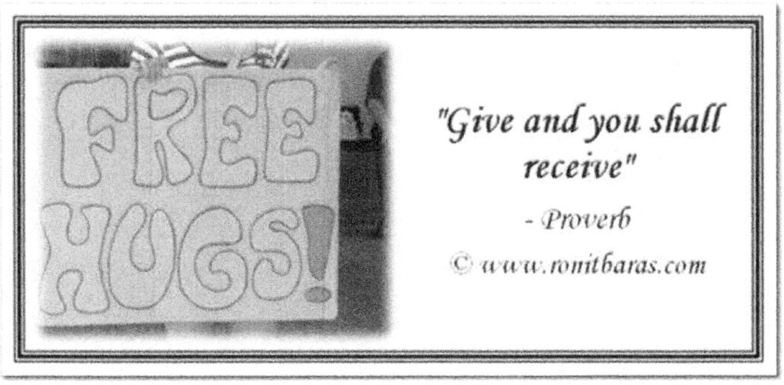
FREE
HUGS!
"Give and you shall receive"
- Proverb
© www.ronitbaras.com

- "Every day is the first day of the rest of my life. I **cherish every day** of my life and look forward to a better, brighter future"

Tips for teaching kids gratitude

1. Teach your kids to look forward. The simple act of looking up will get them started (that is the way the brain is "wired").

2. Pay attention to how you talk. When you blame, justify and analyze the past, you are looking backwards. Look up...

3. When your kids face difficulties, be with them and help them move on.

4. Pick quotes of courage and positive mindset and repeat them over and over again.

5. Help your kids imagine a brighter future. Sometimes, they cannot do it by themselves. Tell them, *"I can imagine you…"*

⌘ **"I think for myself**. I know that in every situation, **I have a choice**. I know that smart choices are choices that are good for me and that do not hurt anyone, including myself"

Tips for developing kids' independent thinking

1. Teaching kids to think for themselves is not easy, because it might mean they might disagree with you, but it is well worth the risk!

2. When you need to make up your mind, ask your kids for advice. This will help them think for themselves.

3. When this does not put them at risk, encourage your kids to think differently.

4. Tell your kids they are unique and special any time you get a chance.

5. Teach your kids to question authority (gently…).

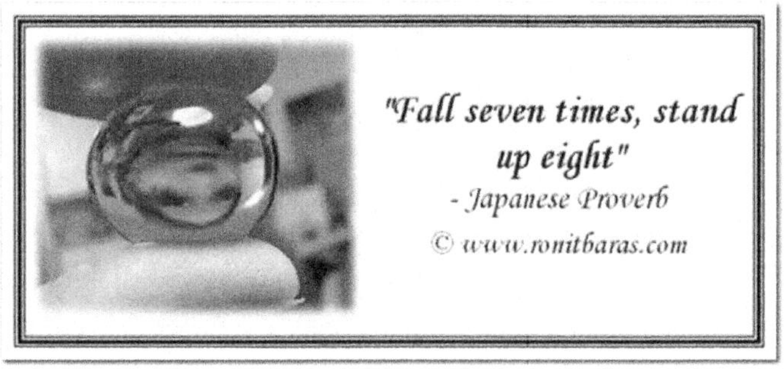
"Fall seven times, stand up eight"
- Japanese Proverb
© www.ronitbaras.com

⌘ "**Actions speak louder than words**. I do not wait for things to happen to me. I do all I can to make them happen the way I want them to. I am a person of action. I move forward with my actions"

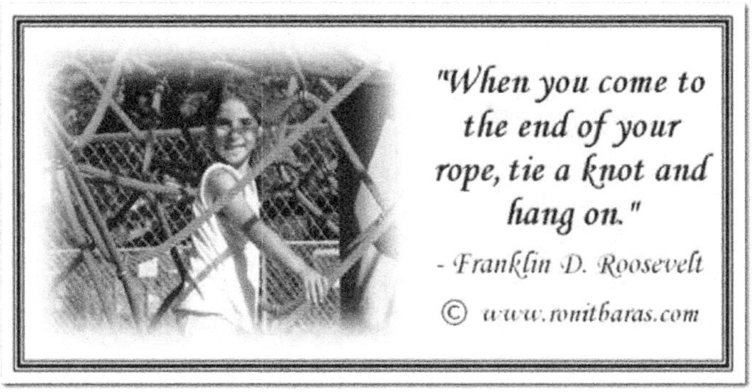
"When you come to the end of your rope, tie a knot and hang on."
- Franklin D. Roosevelt
© www.ronitbaras.com

- "Life is a learning journey. **I learn something every day"**

Tips for supporting learning

1. At the end of every day, ask your kids, *"What have you learned today?"*

- "If I do not know something, **I can always learn"**

Tips for motivating kids to learn

1. Make sure your kids separate school learning from personal growth.
2. Tell your kids about things you have learned every day.
3. Once a year, encourage your kids to write "100 things I have learned in my life" (start with 10 and work your way up to 100 with age).
4. Share your life's lessons with your kids and write your own list.

- "I am being **polite** when I wait for my turn and **say "please" and "thank you"**"

Tips for promoting politeness

1. Say, *"please"* when you ask anyone (including your kids) for something, even if it is just passing the salt.
2. Say *"thank you"* when anyone does something for you, even if it is just passing the salt.

- **"Everyone makes mistakes, so instead of getting angry with myself, I try to do a bit better every time"**

Tips for encouraging small stretches

1. Focus on small stretches and progress not on the end result.
2. Explain to kids that guilt and shame are very debilitating feelings and it is better to do things differently.

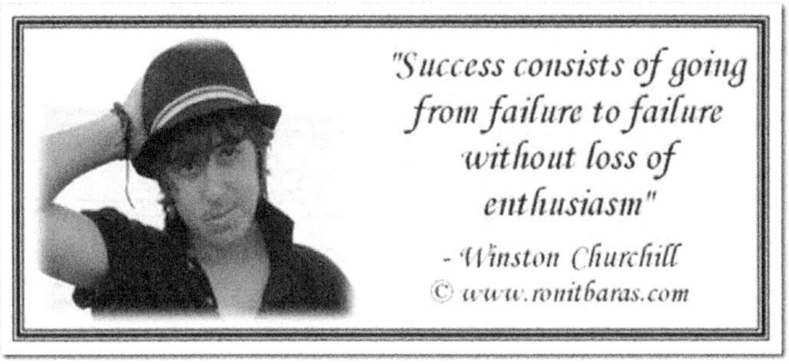
"Success consists of going from failure to failure without loss of enthusiasm"
- Winston Churchill
© www.ronitbaras.com

- **"Smiling is contagious**. I smile at everyone. I smile at the bus driver, at my teachers and at people on the street. When I smile, others smile back, and the world becomes a happier place"

- "I never ever hurt myself**. I take good care of my body and my mind"**

- **"There are some things that are important to me and I do not compromise on them to gain others' love and attention"**

Tips for encouraging assertiveness and critical thinking

1. Talk to your kids about what is important to them.
2. Talk to your kids about peer pressure.
3. Pay attention to your own actions that show you are succumbing to peer pressure, such as lifestyle decisions (car, decorations and clothes) and social "obligations".

- **"When I start something, I finish it"**

Tips for encouraging persistence

1. Again, pay attention to the process and do not be fussy about the end result.

- "If I stop and **think before I do things**. I know I will do the right thing. I know what the right thing is. I only need to follow my heart"

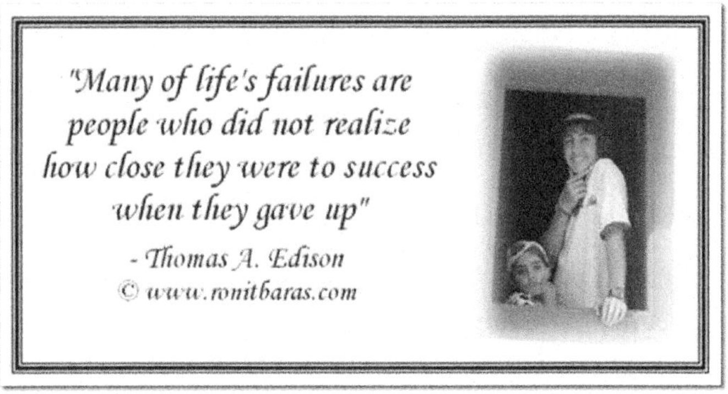
"Many of life's failures are people who did not realize how close they were to success when they gave up"
- Thomas A. Edison
© www.ronitbaras.com

✄ "I am a person of integrity. **When I promise to do something, I do it** (as long as I do not hurt myself or others)

✄ **"When I share what I have with others, I have more of it"**

✄ **"I always take care of myself and when offered to take part in illegal things, I am confident enough to say 'No'"**

✄ **"I do not take what is not mine.** I respect other's rights and property"

Tips for promoting honesty

1.   Teaching honesty and integrity takes time, effort, and most of all a good example. Be a role model – never take what is not yours.

2.   Never look at your kids' stuff without permission.

3.   Reward your kids for returning what is not theirs.

✄ **"I never, never, never give up.** I keep trying until I achieve what I want. Determination is the highest quality of successful people. I am successful. I follow the rules and try to make my home/school/community a better place"

✄ **"When I have a problem, I strive for a solution.** I try not to hurt others on my way to the solution"

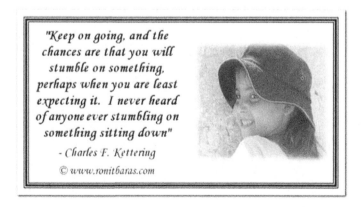

"Keep on going, and the chances are that you will stumble on something, perhaps when you are least expecting it. I never heard of anyone ever stumbling on something sitting down"
- Charles F. Kettering
© www.ronitbaras.com

✄ **"Creativity is a peak state.** I am creative when I paint, write, dance, play music, draw or do any form of art"

Tips for developing your kids' creativity

1.   Embrace your kids' different attitude. Every time your kids do things that are different from the majority, even strange, remember that the most creative people in history were different before they became great.

2. Allow your kids to choose their own clothes. Let them put food on their own plate. Encourage them to decorate their own room or schoolbag and to express what they love.

3. Teach your kids to question, to doubt and encourage them to do things better than you. When you tell them your opinion, say it as your opinion only and let them know you understand other people do things differently and they can still be happy and successful even if they choose a different way. Ask your kids for their opinion and express respect towards what they think even when they do not think like you.

4. Avoid promoting perfectionism. Perfectionism is a disease transmitted from parents to kids and it kills creativity.

✖ **"I can change** if I want to. **Change is easy.** I only need to choose"

"Thousands of candles can be lit from a single candle, and the life of the candle will not be shortened. Happiness never decreases by being shared"
- Buddha
© www.ronitbaras.com

✖ **"I am Responsible,** and my parents can **trust** me to do the right thing"

Tips for teaching responsibility and trust

1. Responsibility is something kids learn. They are not born with it. Define responsibility for your kids so they do not have to guess what you expect of them.

2. Always remember that blaming and justifying are the enemies of responsibility.

3. Make sure your kids do not confuse blaming themselves with taking responsibility. Responsibility means learning and moving forward.

4. Start early. Even a 3-year-old can be responsible for taking his/ her plate off the table after a meal.

5. Make sure you do all of it gradually and as appropriate to the age of your kids.

6. Chores are a good way to teach responsibility. Have a list of age-appropriate chores and make sure you are clear about the reward

attached (make sure you reward effort and not end result and stay away from punishments).

7. Tell your kids that responsibility builds trust between parents and kids. If they behave in a responsible way, you will trust them more.

- **"I can always say 'No'** when someone asks me to do something that I am not completely sure I want to do"

Tips for developing safety and critical thinking

1. These may be hard for you to instill as you want your kids to follow you blindly, but it is better to have these beliefs then for your kids to be easily subject to pressure, especially when your kids are a grown up.

2. Teach your kids to evaluate their own choices and decisions and to trust their instincts. Instinct is not a 100% bullet proof mechanism but it better than following someone else's ship. Even if that someone else is you.

- "It is normal to have good and bad feelings. Bad feelings go away eventually"

- "**Everyone has the same 24 hours a day**. Some people use them wisely and others waste them. I learn to manage my time and when I manage it well, I can find the time to do everything I want to do"

Tips for helping kids with their time management

1. Encourage your kids to have a diary.

2. Encourage your kids to plan ahead.

3. Teach your kids to work to a schedule.

4. Have a family calendar to teach your kids to consider other people's plans and time tables.

5. Hang your kids' school time tables in a visible place for everyone to see.

- "**I know I am going to be successful. What I believe will come true**. I will keep believing it until I am successful"

- "**I eat healthy food because my body is important to me**"

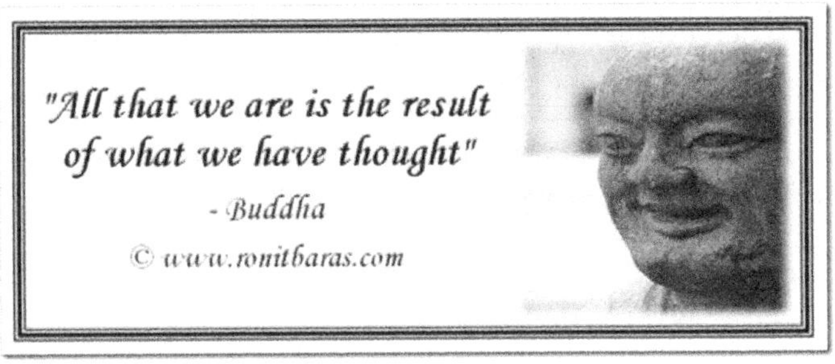
"All that we are is the result of what we have thought"
- Buddha
© www.ronitbaras.com

"I care about the world I live in and I keep it clean"

Tips for motivating kids to care for their environment

1. Caring for the world we live in is a higher state of being. We can adapt our parenting style to motivate our kids to make a difference in the world they live in by being a role model.

2. Below are 55 ways to make a difference in the world. Each one can become an affirmation. I am sure some will be more appealing than others. Tell your kids that they make a difference in the world just by being. They certainly make a difference in your life just by being.

3. Talk about making a difference in the immediate world, because not everything involves giving money to poor people. Turning off the light or helping out is much more real to kids.

4. Pick 3 ideas you can do with your kids. Ask for their opinion and, most importantly, ask them why these are good things to do and make sure they know the reasons.

Ideas for making a difference in the world

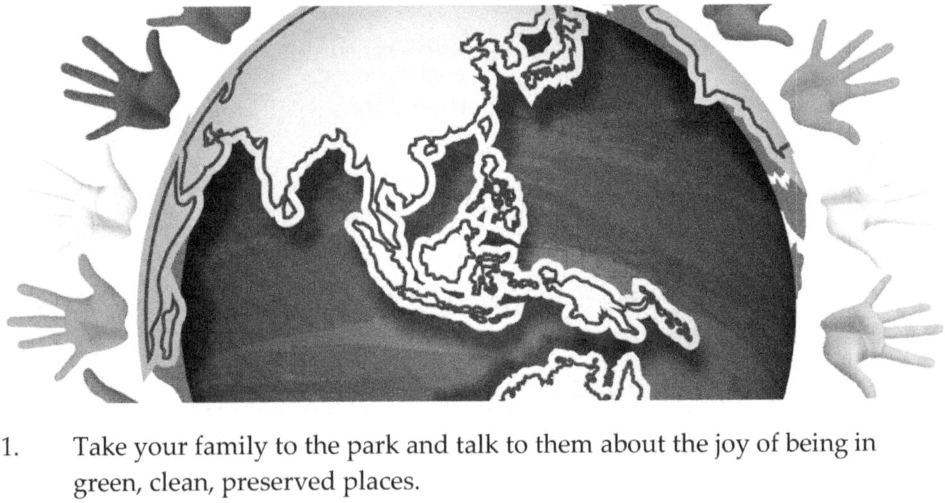

1. Take your family to the park and talk to them about the joy of being in green, clean, preserved places.

2. When you are outside, clean up after yourself and teach your kids that just as they do not litter at home, they should act the same way in our "global home".

3. Plant a garden and teach your kids to care for the garden. If you live in an apartment building, have pot plants and take care of them. Kids get really excited when they see plants grow, make flowers and bear fruit.

4. Every year, plant new things in your garden and teach your kids about plant rotation.

5. When you go camping, put out your fire properly. Be careful with cigarettes and fire in the bush.

6. Set up a compost bin and put your organic waste in it. Show your kids how the compost helps your garden grow.

7. When you fish, follow the fishing rules. The rules are there to protect the fish, but in the long term, they protect the people.

8. Turn off the lights when they are not needed.

9. Avoid long showers.

10. Use water-saving appliances. Consider the water rating before you buy.

11. Walk instead of driving.

12. Ride a bike instead of driving.

13. Walk up the stairs instead of using the elevator or escalator (it will make you healthier too).

14. Car pool if you can.

15. Use public transport if you can.

16. Install a "half flush" in your toilet.

17. Open your car windows from time to time (in good air) to connect with the outside and save the energy needed for air conditioning.

18. Hang your clothes outside to dry instead of using a dryer.

19. Use your washing machine only when you have a full load.

20. Use your dishwasher only when you have a full load.

21. Use solar power and solar water heating.

22. Recycle your clothes. Donate them or use their fabric to make something else. The more you use, the less everyone needs to produce.

23. Separate your garbage and recycle.

24. Buy products with less wrapping and packaging.

25. Use reusable bags and boxes instead of plastic bags.

26. Do not print things you do not have to. Adjust your computer applications to make text easy to read.

27. Use recycled paper.

28. Print on both sides of the page if possible.

29. Use emails as much as you can to save printing.

30. Pay your bills online (and choose to receive email statements) to save trees and reduce carbon emissions.

31. Be careful what you wash down the sink (avoid disposing of oil, paint or hazardous chemicals).

32. Use a strainer and/or garbage disposer in your sink.

33. Plan your shopping. If you buy more than you need and have to throw it away, everybody loses.

34. Use leftover food to make new dishes.

35. Turn off taps and make sure they do not leak.

36. Find ways to save water in your shower, toilet, garden and sink.

37. Wash your car on the grass.

38. Use energy-efficient light bulbs (they are everywhere now, and they produce warm light and last for years).

39. Reuse your food containers, but do not use them in the microwave oven (they're not suitable).

40. Buy in bulk to save on packaging.

41. When you use your oven, avoid opening the door.

42. When you heat water, heat only as much as you need.

43. When you bake, try to do all your baking in one go, so you only have to preheat the oven once.

44. Clean all your filters.

45. Use timers for electric appliances.

46. When you mow your lawn, use the cuttings for compost.

47. Borrow equipment you rarely use from other people instead of buying new ones

48. Lend other people your equipment, too.

49. Find natural alternatives for chemical cleaners.

50. Reuse envelopes.

51. Use old magazines and phone books for arts and craft.

52. Avoid using disposable plates, cups and cutlery.

53. If you can work from home (or very close to home), do it.

54. Buy used furniture.

55. Try to fix things before you buy new ones.

⌘ "**My safety is important**. Before I do something, I ask myself, "Is it safe?""

Tips for creating awareness to danger

1. Safety is probably something that is very important for every parent. Do not try to teach your kids about safety when things are stressful, and they cannot understand how they can feel different. Talk about it when everything is OK and everyone is all right.

2. Talk to your kids about stranger danger. No need to say that every stranger is dangerous. It is better to say, *"If you don't know someone, don't take a risk"*. Check out the book The Berenstain Bears Learn about Strangers for inspiration.

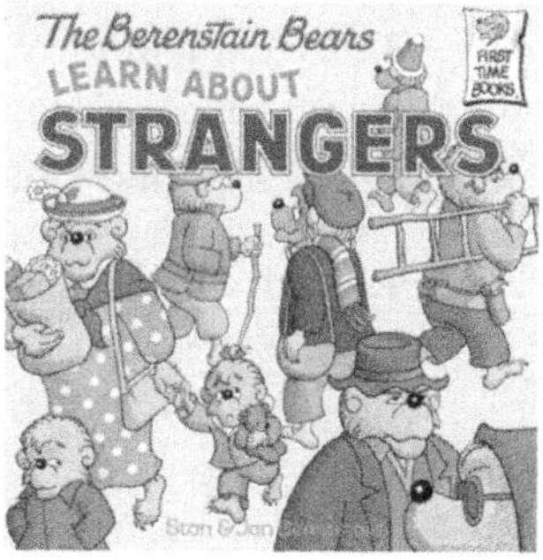

3. Talk to your kids about internet safety.

4. Teach your kids to trust their gut instincts if they feel something is wrong and encourage them to stay away from people who give them that feeling.

5. Pay attention to what you say danger is. Make sure you do not overuse the word. If your kids think you are saying that simple, harmless things are dangerous, they will not trust you anymore (you cry "Wolf!").

6. Make sure your kids understand what an immediate threat is and what is not. Some kids may think that the talks about global warming are a daily threat on their life, so it is better to discuss it as a future possibility that we can do all that we can to change, but is not likely to affect us today, next week or even next year.

7. Stay away from associating danger with a particular group of people. You could be creating another problem that way.

✕ **"Every time I look in the mirror, I say something good to the person I see in it".**

✕ **"Every day, I ask myself, "What can I do today to make this day a wonderful day?" and try to achieve it."**

✕ "Everything I need in order to succeed is here around me. I only need to see it".

✕ **"I have the courage to stand up for my beliefs".**

✕ **"I do not take risks that can be too dangerous and hurt myself or others".**

Tips for promoting critical thinking and evaluating risk

1. Living life involves taking risks. Make sure your kids do not think that risks are bad. Explain that every new thing you try involves the risk of not succeeding, but that should not stop anyone from trying anyway.

2. Talk to your kids about the pros and cons of everything they consider. It is a good strategy to have.

3. Explain to your kids that people are not fortune tellers. We never know what the outcome of our actions will be for sure, but we should still follow our dreams.

4. Explain to your kids about risks that cannot be reversed, like using some drugs or getting into dangerous situations with no safety measures. This should definitely be strong enough in their mind to stop them from getting hurt.

✕ **"I am unique and special.** There is no one else like me in the entire world. I do not have to wear certain clothes, behave a certain way or do anything in particular to be unique. If I am myself then that is my uniqueness".

> *"When you feel like giving up,*
> *remember why you held on for so*
> *long in the first place"*
> - *Unknown*
> © *www. ronitbaras.com*

Exercise: Affirmation starters

If you want to know the thoughts or feelings your kids **want to have** and would like to motivate them through positive affirmations, encourage them to complete the relevant sentences from the list below.

You may find they cannot come up with a positive statement. This is a good opportunity for you to pay more attention to that statement, encourage them to find positive alternatives or talk to them about that particular area.

As always, do this activity yourself first to discover the messages you may be sending to your kids.

1.   A good memory from my childhood is

2.   The best gift I was given was

3.   In the past, I used to

4.   Family for me is

5.   What I really want is

6.   I dream that one day I will

7.   Life will be better when

8.   I am very special when

9.   The things I am willing to do to feel good are

10.   I want people to remember me like

11.   I believe that one day I will be

12.   My greatest strength is

13.   My mom is proud of me for

14.   I want to believe that

15. I consider myself lucky because

16. I hope that one day I will

17. I am focused when

18. A good trait I took from dad is

19. When I feel happy, I

20. My favorite food is

21. My best skill is

22. My most valuable possession is

23. If I die, the thing I would like people to know about me is

24. The thing that makes me smile is

25. My dad is proud of me for

26. One thing I must do before I die is

27. I want to choose friends that make me feel

28. A good trait I took from mom is

29. The thing that really makes me happy is

30. I want my life to be

31. I am very proud of myself for

32. What I love about myself is

33. I cry out of joy when

34. I choose to feel good about myself because

35. I'm happy when

36. I am very talented in

37. I am kind when

38. I am very confident when

39. The bravest thing I ever did was

40. It's OK to

41. I feel courageous when

42.   I like friends who are

43.   I like it when

44.   I consider myself successful because

45.   I appreciate myself for

46.   I love myself because

47.   I trust myself to

Summary

✓   Affirmations are a **good way to encourage your kids** to move forward.

✓   Affirmations are **thoughts carved in your kids' minds** that will be used as navigating tool when you are not around. They are the statements the parrots sitting on their shoulders will repeat for years.

✓   **Parents are gardeners**. Whatever they say and the way they act becomes a seed and it will grow. It can either be a happy flower or a flower with thorns. It will either bear nutritious or poisonous fruits. Your choice!

✓   The chatter in our head is a self-talk mechanism that **either encourages us to do things or warn us off doing something.** It can keep us from danger or from progress. It is parent's desire to make sure the chatter box uses positive, encouraging, courageous, self-esteem boosting affirmations.

✓   Most of the affirmations we use are thoughts we collected as kids from people who are close to us and from past experiences. It is best to **watch what you're saying** rather than have to replace bad thoughts.

✓ There are two ways to instill affirmations: **modeling and saying**. For both you need to be consistent and use repetition and they must be in sync with each other.

✓ The best way to instill affirmations is to **evaluate yours as a parent** and make a conscious choice which ones you need to get rid of and which affirmations you wish to plant in your kids' navigation garden and water. Remember, every thought, belief and quote are affirmations and will grow.

✓ **Motivating your kids is like giving them a fish, while teaching them to motivate themselves is like giving them a fishing net**. Pick the affirmations you like and focus on carving them in your kids' mind. Saying them is not enough; you have to model and repeat it them. How long? As long as it takes.

17 CHAPTER SEVENTEEN

EXTERNAL INFLUENCES AND SUSTAINABILITY

In the process of motivating your kids, you will find that your kids are also influenced by others. If that influence is positive – great! But sometimes, others' behavior and words might be de-motivating for your kids.

Although parental influences are typically the strongest in a child's life, parents may face challenges cleaning up bad effects created by other sources. After all, keeping kids at home, away from all the other people who might tell them they cannot succeed or expose them to stories of despair and failure is virtually impossible.

So, what can parents do?

First, you need to be aware of the various sources of information and pressure in your kids' life and focus on balancing them with your own values. Bear in mind, some influences cannot be eliminated, such as partners who do not share your attitude, siblings with a negative outlook and other family members you cannot stop seeing. Instead of saying bad things about those people, try to emphasize the others who present the right attitude and behavior.

Research done on parents discovered that kids will be drawn to the more positive parent so if you want to make sure your kids follow you, be positive.

Exercise: Discover the Naysayers

To deal with your kids' de-motivators, you need to identify who they are and what they do to de-motivate your kids:

Make a list of all your kids' influencers – family members, friends, teachers, teammates, playmates and so on.

Rate their influence on your kids (from 1-10) – in terms of motivation, how positive are they and how important is their opinion (1 is low and 10 is high)?

Ask your kids to rate their influence as well. You will be surprised to discover that what you think is not the same as theirs.

Compare what you think about those peoples' influence and what your kids think about it. Every contradiction in your perception is a problem because it is hard to motivate kids and help them if you are not on the same page.

Order the list with strong and very negative influencers at the top. Unimportant and positive people can be taken off (Don't get rid of the positive people, keep them in mind and encourage your kids to associate with them but for the purpose of this exercise we focus only on those who de-motivate and are strong influencers).

Discuss with your kids how those people contribute to their life in a good way and how they contribute in a "not so good" way. Guide your kids by asking age-appropriate questions that will help them recall and classify behaviors and events. Try not to push your own agenda.

Counter de-motivating influences by providing positive examples and linking them to positive results and happiness. For example, if one of your kids has a "cool" friend who refuses to practice playing the piano, give an example of someone else who practices happily and succeeds, while still being "cool" (Harry Connick Jr? Stevie Wonder? Alicia Keys?).

Did you know?

Research done on parents discovered that kids will be drawn to the more positive parent. Many parents are in conflict with partners on parenting strategies. If you want to make sure your kids will follow you, be positive.

Tips for making the influencer list

✓ When making a list of influencers, you can do the same exercise on yourself (did you see that one coming?). Ask who has influenced your own life? Start with the family circle, teachers, friends and even neighbors. You are likely to find influences you had never thought about.

✓ Comparing ratings will give you an indication of the difference between your perception and your kids'. No one is right! It is just a perception.

✓ If you think someone is de-motivating your kids, ask them, *"Do you think this is a good thing to do/say?"* Sometimes, this question alone will do the trick.

✓ Keep telling your kids you want them to hang around people who will make them feel and think highly of themselves and motivate them to be the best they can be. It may help them think of some of their relationships that are not so healthy for them.

✓ Bear in mind you cannot eliminate some influences at all. Bad mouthing that person is not a good technique as it pushes your kids to take sides and might leave you on the losing side. Work for your kids' good, not against anybody else. Guide your kids towards their own "Aha" moments and let them make their own changes.

Usually, finding the de-motivators and their methods is a good way of finding what works on your kids. For example, if someone puts them down with words, you can use the praise and appreciation techniques to counter that. If they are influenced by people who give them gifts, you can counter that with your own rewards.

Self-motivation and sustainability

The main aim in motivating your kids is to make them think self-motivating thoughts by themselves, which will ensure they will be able to find strength within themselves to move forward. Here is a quote I love very much by Marianne Williamson, which expresses the challenges of adopting self-motivating thoughts. This can be great inspiration for kids and grownups alike. I have it posted in many places in the house and I have put a copy of it in each of my kids' albums.

If your ship doesn't come, swim to it

– Jonathan Winters

"Our deepest fear is not that we are inadequate. Our deepest fear is that we are powerful beyond measure. It is our light, not our darkness that most frighten us. We ask ourselves, 'who am I to e brilliant, gorgeous, talented and fabulous?'

Actually, who are you not to be? You are a child of God. Your playing small doesn't serve the world. There is nothing enlightened about shrinking so that other people won't feel insecure around you.

We are all meant to shine, as children do. We are born to make manifest the glory of God that is within us. It's not just in some of us, it's in everyone. And as we let our own light shine, we unconsciously give other people permission to do the same as we are liberated from our own fear, our presence automatically liberates others"

- Marianne Williamson

www.ronitbaras.com

I'm proud of me!

From a very early stage, kids learn to be modest and because they do not fully understand the meaning of modesty, kids confuse being proud with being arrogant. Therefore, they find it hard to have happy, positive thoughts about themselves in fear of being seen as condescending. Believe it or not, most people would rather think low of themselves than be considered arrogant.

I would like to share with you something that happened in a leadership camp I run every year. It was an amazing example of how hard it is for kids (and grownups) to be proud of themselves and why it is important to change that attitude.

Every year, I take a group of student leaders in grade six and seven from seven schools to an intensive, two days leadership camp. As part of the camp, I ask their parents to write their kids an "I believe in you letter" and give it to the kids on the first night as a surprise.

In previous camps and workshops in schools, I had noticed that kids did not display a sense of pride in themselves. They talked freely about being proud of a team they admired in sport, but had quite a different attitude towards being proud of themselves, their family or their class.

In the first hour of camp, I asked each of the kids and the teachers to introduce themselves and then to tell the group something about themselves they were proud of. Everyone, kids and adults, looked at me in surprise.

Recognizing one's own feelings is the basic level of emotional intelligence, so I thought that when we addressed leadership, recognizing things I am good at as a starter would be a good way for the kids to start appreciating their strengths. I was surprised to see how much easier it was for kids (and grownups) to talk about things they were not proud of, as if they had practiced those so much, they came to them naturally.

Most of the kids struggled with the idea of being proud. I pushed them by giving an example. I said, "*I'm Ronit (we were still getting to know one another) and I'm very proud of myself for organizing this camp*". Some shy kids said hesitantly they were proud of themselves for having been chosen to be in this camp, but most of them said they did not know what to say. They used words like "boasting" and "bragging", being "full of themselves" and "arrogant" as the reasons they could not find anything they were proud of.

"The drops of rain make a hole in the stone not by violence but by soft falling"
- *Lucretius*
© www.ronitbaras.com

In the evening, straight after dinner, I gave the kids their letters. They were shocked, some started crying and all of them were very emotional. At one stage, I asked, *"Who wants to read his/her letter out loud?"* and Beth said she preferred Jessica to read her letter because it was embarrassing to read aloud good things about herself. I decided to discuss pride with the kids. (By the way, I want you to know I have been doing this for many years, it sounds the same every year)

"It's like I'm bragging", Beth said.

"Why is it like bragging?" I asked her.

"I don't know", said Beth, "It's like I'm showing off that my mother loves me".

"What is showing off?" I asked and pointed my question at the other students.

"It's when you make someone feel bad", said someone.

"No, it's not", said someone else, "Why would anyone feel bad if Beth's mom loves her?"

(This is when I love my job. When they talk to each other and sort out their perception on their own)

"Some people may feel bad if their mom didn't say she loved them", suggested another child.

"But it's not Beth's fault", was the answer.

"But this is the truth. Beth's mom wrote her a love letter and Beth is very happy. I think she can share it", said another student.

I asked them, "If you're proud and happy that your mom loves you, is that bragging?"

"Yes".

"No".

"You can be proud, but you don't have to talk about it".

"Why not?"

"In case someone feels bad".

"It's not fair. It means I can't say anything good about myself, in case someone else feels bad".

I said, "That means I cannot be proud of myself for organizing this camp".

"You can", said someone, "Because it doesn't say anything bad about anyone else".

We continued this discussion for a while, until the kids concluded that saying something good about yourself and at the same time saying something bad about someone else was being "full of yourself" and "bragging", but saying something good about yourself without mention of others was being proud.

One compromise was to call it "sharing". If you share something good someone says about you it is not completely bragging and because (Thank Goodness!) they all had love letters, no one would feel bad listening to other students' love letters from their parents.

As the kids read some of their letters out loud, I knew there was lots of work I still needed to do. The school principal who attended the camp, told the kids he had won a very special award and that even he felt uncomfortable talking about it fearing someone might think he was being arrogant, but he said that during the day of camp, he had realized it was OK to be proud and say good things about yourself and that leaders needed to learn to accept compliments from others.

It was very late, so I told the students to go to bed and instead of turning off the lights; I went to each room and told them about my family ceremony every night.

"Before we go to bed, we ask ourselves two questions, 'What was a special thing that happened to me today?' and 'What am I proud of today?'" I gave them time to think and they all gave me their answers with confidence. Compared to what they had said in the morning, their answers were amazingly different. While in the morning they had tried to convince me that being proud was bragging, each of them came up with something great to say at night.

"I'm proud of myself for sleeping away from home".

"I'm proud of myself for sharing my letter".

"I'm proud to be my dad's son".

"I'm proud to be part of this camp".

"I'm proud of making new friends".

"I'm proud of myself for making the Athletics team" (there was someone in every room who was proud of winning in sport or going up a level).

"I'm proud of being a good brother to my sister".

"I'm proud of being a good student".

"I'm proud of helping my mom with my baby sister".

"I'm proud that I speak to my parents in another language".

"I'm proud of my family".

Only 16 hours had passed since the morning when I asked the kids to say things they were proud of, and they told me with confident, happy smiles a huge list of things they were proud of. Only 16 hours … and a letter later…

I have been in the business of facilitating change for over 30 years. People tell me it takes years to make a change. I say it takes hours and with the right guidance, we can make a huge difference to our children, our students and to the whole of society.

Kids, who are proud of themselves, have permission to motivate themselves when they aim for their goals, when they want to stretch themselves, when they take risks and need to overcome obstacles.

Self-pride is the most sustainable motivating tool that will last forever. "I am proud of me!" is the affirmation you want to hear your kids saying, because this is the proof they can motivate themselves. This is when you know you have accomplished what you wanted and more, because they will be able to fill their confidence tank by themselves and be happy. You wanted to give them a fish and you have taught them to fish using a fishing net.

"Having children makes you no more a parent than having a piano makes you a pianist"

- Michael Levine

© www.ronitbaras.com

How long is long enough?

You are probably asking yourself, *"How long will I have to motivate my kids for?"* The answer is probably, *"For the rest of your life"*. However, you may not need to do much when your kids are grownups and can fill up their own bowls of praise and self-appreciation. You will not have to work that hard when they surround themselves with people who share the same values as you and who will be able to motivate and support them even when you are not around.

When your kids have the right people around them, coupled with the right attitude and skills to motivate themselves, you can relax and be certain you have put them on the right path.

When my kids say, *"I was very proud of myself today"*, I know I have done a good job as a parent. Teach your kids to use this affirmation so they can hear this sentence in their own voice and know it is accepted and legitimate.

First, give your kids some "fish" – love, care, happy experiences and encouragement to make sure they will survive. Then, teach them how to fish using a fishing net – encourage them to love themselves, to care for themselves and to give themselves happy experiences.

Only when you reach that second level does your motivation become sustainable!

Summary

- ✓ Find your kids influencers and pick the de-motivators. Try, if you can, to keep them away from those de-motivators. It takes much longer to uproot a poisonous plant than to grow a flower plant.

- ✓ Compare what you think about those influencers with your kids' perception

- ✓ Work with your kids on recognizing whether an influence is good for them or not

- ✓ Find out your own influencers and de-motivators. Be honest!

- ✓ Counter de-motivation with encouragement and positive, motivating ideas and never bad-mouth others

- ✓ Your motivation is sustainable when your kids can motivate themselves through appreciation and self-pride.

✓ Kids and adults confuse pride and bragging, boasting and being "full of yourself". They naturally talk about what they are ashamed of but find it hard to share achievements and receive compliments. This limits their ability to motivate themselves.

✓ Teach the difference between arrogance and pride and encourage them to be proud of themselves. It does not take long to change a child's perception. Don't say it. Help them learn it through questioning the belief "It is bad to be proud".

✓ Adopt ceremonies of pride and be a role model of pride. Dinners, car rides, bed times are good opportunities to share pride.

✓ Kids who are proud of themselves and express it give themselves the permission to motivate themselves. This is when you know you have mastered the art of motivating your kids.

✓ How long will have to do it? As long as it takes until you hear the sentence "I am proud of me".

"I think with this key,

I can go everywhere"

– Dalai Lama

FINAL WORDS AND SUMMARY

Motivating kids is an art. Unfortunately, having kids and parenting them is not enough to master this art. Motivating your kids requires taking responsibility for your kids' motivation and making a commitment to keep learning and improving your motivational skills to an art form. If we need 10,000 hours to mastery, we better make good use of every second we spend with them.

What you need to remember is that if you try each and every exercise presented to you in this book, you will surely find the best way to motivate your own kids. Success lies in the combination of your kids' personalities and needs with yours.

I hope I have managed to convey the message that **you are the key!** What you think, what you feel and what you need are very important to your success in motivating your kids to be happy, healthy and successful in life.

I can reassure you that many parents manage to make huge changes in their relationships with their kids by using only a single activity from what I have presented here. If you think it takes a long time to make a change, please know that most of the times, it is hard to recognize the change, but nevertheless, the change occurs.

If you look at your reflection in the mirror, you may not be able to see your changes, but if you take a photo of yourself and look at it in 3 months, you will be able to see the change clearly. This is why I recommend measuring the progress in your ability to motivate your kids. You will be surprised to find out how much has changed if you just focus on it.

Motivating is a skill you are not born with but can develop. In this book, you will find the ultimate guide to become the best motivational parent. I hope reading motivated you to become that parent.

I have included a summary of all chapters to remind you of the "how to" of the motivating art.

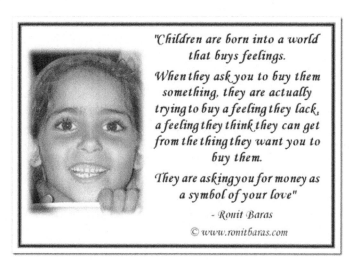

"Children are born into a world that buys feelings.

When they ask you to buy them something, they are actually trying to buy a feeling they lack, a feeling they think they can get from the thing they want you to buy them.

They are asking you for money as a symbol of your love"

- Ronit Baras

© www.ronitbaras.com

Chapter 1: Parenting, Coaching and Motivation

Parents are the **best potential motivators** as they are the most important agents of socialization.

Parents and coaches are givers. **The parent as a coach** is the best approach in motivating children and directing them to a desired outcome. A coaching relationship is personalized, focused, includes respect and is supportive and motivating.

To allow motivation to happen, kids need to do most of the talking and parents have to be **"kind listeners"** and in control of their own feelings.

Games are a wonderful tool for learning. Use the **"fun Incentive"** to motivate your child.

Chapter 2: Motivation, sailing and war

We are all sailing in the sea of life with captain (conscious) crew (subconscious) and Max (the little voice). The direction we take in life depends on the maps our crew has.

In order to change direction and motivate ourselves or our kids **we must work on the subconscious** with focus and clarity and convince our crew that it is safe to do so. Pressure only makes our subconscious resist the change.

If a change only lasts 3 days or in best cases a week, it is a sign we **did not include our crew** in the planning of our journey, and we are de-motivated. Next time, we would need more time to try again.

Each of us has a **separate ship** and while kids are dragged by their parents' ship, their crew is constantly working towards independence. Don't fight it. It is a healthy process. One day, they will sail on their own guided by their own captains and crew. You have a window of opportunity during childhood to help them develop safe maps and very supportive parrots.

Do not plant negative orders (fear) in your kids' parrot or try to add them to their map. Picture a positive future so when you are not there, their Max will be your extension in times of trouble whispering, "you can!"

The war between the captain and crew will be there forever. The more we work on the relationship between the two, the easier it will be for us to get what we want.

Chapter 3: What is Motivation?

All parents want to motivate their kids. Do not fall into the trap of saying, "*I accept everything my kids do*", because if it were true, you would not be reading this book. No one brings kids to the world to let them find out by themselves (the hard way) how to be healthy, successful and happy.

Your definition of motivation is crucial. Motivating is not encouraging your kids to do what you want, but to do what **they** want.

Self-interview is a wonderful way to get to know your subconscious. Help your kids get to know their subconscious too by interviewing them.

If you want to encourage kids to be, do, or have something they want, you must **first find out what they want**. Ask!

Ask without assumptions and judgment and do not use it as a test. Be a kind listener.

If you want your kids to want a lot (which will guarantee they will have more of everything) **encourage them to dream and dream big!**

Chapter 4: Chunking down

Kids have a challenge with responsibility when they feel overwhelmed. This is natural, so be understanding to their desire to transfer responsibility to you. Your expectations must be suitable to their age, to their abilities and to the situation. Do not be tempted to do things for them.

Teach your kids to **chunk down and focus on small goals.** Even grownups feel overwhelmed when they have no idea how to handle a situation. It is just normal. Focusing on smaller bits is always a good way to lower the stress level. Three months is long enough to aim for. Adjust the wait to their age and help them accumulate success stories.

"Fairy land" is our outlet to manage failure and disappointment. It is natural and we can stay there for a short time, but it is disempowering.

Trying again and again, even if we fail, teaches us something that may be useful next time.

Help your kids do something to achieve what they want. **They must take action to get there.** Waiting for success to fall from the sky is one of the main causes of people's struggles in our society – they feel helpless. Even when opportunity knocks, you must open the door for it to come in.

Emphasize the process, not the end result. When you are too focused on end results, you risk raising "perfectionists" and overcoming that is harder than overcoming lack of motivation. Make sure they understand that movement forward is the success.

Understand that your encouragements are suggestions only and **it is your kids' right to choose to take or not to take your advice.** Forcing them to accept your help is not helpful. In fact, it destroys their motivation.

Chapter 5: Carrots and Sticks

It is only human to be **motivated by pain and pleasure**. This is how we form a self-concept of right and wrong. We are programmed to take our hands away from the burning fire to make sure we survive.

Carrots are better than sticks. Sticks cause pain and unfortunately, after we have learned the "lesson" the pain is still there. Some stick's pain lasts a long time. Every sofa in the psychologists or therapist's clinic has heard stories of pain from sticks echoing 50-60 years later.

Don't use sticks too often. Inflation in using sticks will make them less effective.

Kids asking help is a sign of you being a trustworthy parent. If kids do not share their problems with you in order to avoid your stick (some words are truly more painful than physical sticks), you have lost your power to parent them and have good influence on them. This is when you risk them seeking help in places that may not be good for them and make sure their Max is recording statements of defeat, helplessness, fear, doubt and failure.

Motivation is a form of giving and discipline is a form of taking. Make sure you give enough as a parent and keep asking yourself *"is it for me? "What do I want to achieve?" "Am I in a position of lacking now?"* Love, unconditional love, is the answer and gives you much power. Never abuse this power.

Expecting kids to fulfill your expectation and abusing your power to make them do it is a sign you are weak. Gather strength from reflecting on your ultimate fears of your child not following your instructions.

Many times, **kids' behavior reflects the conflicts between parents on forms of discipline/motivation**. One parent thinks discipline is the answer and the other consider this not effective. Avoid using the concept of discipline. If you think of discipline, you are taking, not giving and can't motivate your kids to do anything (other than maybe avoid your company).

Small, gentle pushes are good ways to help kids walk on their own. If you push the kid to walk and he cries and feel pain, it will usually take him longer to stand up and try again. Remember, safety first. Do not risk kids falling on their face.

Chapter 6: The Approval Trap

Kids are born into the approval trap. We use approval as a socializing tool. We can't live totally free from this need but if we can't live without it, we are doomed to be miserable and dependent on what others think of us.

Kids cannot be motivated when they are in the approval trap. We trained them to follow those who give them approval and we can't complain when they follow whoever puts more pressure on them.

Most people are approval addicts. **Approval is very much like a drug.** Unfortunately, most parents are the drug dealers. Our education system is one of the biggest drug dealers in our society and produces lots of addicts craving for just one shot of approval.

Self-reflection is essential to stopping this cycle of the approval trap. **Parents in the approval trap raise kids in the approval trap** who will raise their kids in the approval trap. This cycle can be stopped at any stage and only by parents who make a conscious decision to do things differently. Let go of the desire for power, forgive and accept your own parents for being trapped themselves, forgive and accept your own thoughts and feelings and be the change you want to see.

Notice the **character traits of the approval seekers** (even if it's you): They use vocabulary that seeks permission, significance, they are easily pressured, not assertive, put others before them, jealous, afraid, followers, blame others and competitive. At first, you will notice it in others. It is easy to see others' hump, but later, you'll start noticing when you do it. No matter what you do, if you possess those skills, do not try to pass them to your kids.

There are **25 strategies to get out of the approval trap**. Study them. As I said, each of the strategies can make the shift by itself. Find those you feel more comfortable with and work with them. If you want to measure improvement rate those skills before and after you work on them from 1 -100. Measurement will keep you motivated.

Chapter 7: Praise and Appreciation

Praise and appreciation are the most basic and easiest motivational techniques. They are verbal awards. They are free and easily accessible (if you have a strong emotional intelligence as a parent). Both boys and girls need them and at every age. Use them often. Be honest and don't overdo it. If you get short on ideas, use the list in the chapter about praises.

To make it easy for you to give your kids praise, remember they have a bowl of praises and this bowl has a direct connection to their success in life. Until kids can fill up this bowl by themselves, it is their parents' responsibility to fill it up. **Do not waste a day of your life without telling your kids how much you love them, how much they mean to you and how wonderful they are.** You don't need a special occasion to do that. Do not expect kids to fill up your bowl. They will be able to give back only when theirs is full. 10 praises a day will keep lots of trouble away.

Punishment, expression of disappointment, anger, blame, judgment, ridicule, threats guilt **"steal" confidence from this bowl**. It is an act of taking, not giving. If you want to motivate kids, you need to be in a giving mode not a taking mode.

Praise for effort not ability or intelligence or kids will give up sooner. Don't praise too often. If you use the approval as a prize, they become addicted to the "approval drug". If you flash with the prize too much, you are taming your kids. It is called conditioning and they will use this trick back on you and do nothing unless you promise them a prize. Praise effort, regardless of the outcome. It is important to build their self-esteem even if they have made mistakes.

Praising is a good way to promote persistence. If you want to be successful at the lottery of life, **buy a ticket!**

Persistence is an *"I can do it if I just keep going"* **switch**. It is a brain function that is stimulated by rewarding small stretches. Focus on small stretches and praise them!

It is easy to give when you have enough but more important to give when you are lacking. Catch 22. Even when you are not happy about something, find something good to say. Take time to relax, think and focus on the positive. Keep thinking about the bowl. Even hard situations can be an opportunity to fill up the appreciation bowl.

If you give your kid a fish, he/she can eat for a day, if you teach your kid to fish, he/she can feed himself/herself forever. **Teach your kid to fill up his own bowl of appreciation and you'll guarantee his future.**

Chapter 8: Rewards

Giving rewards is a great way to motivate kids. If you are afraid that your kids *"will get used to it"*, make sure you reward after, not before.

Never use food as rewards. You don't want to raise a child who comforts himself/herself as a grown up with food every time he/she feels bad. Consider outings and eating together as an alternative.

It is better to **prepare a reward list** before you need it. Make sure you agree with your partner on the rewards, so the kids do not "divide and conquer". Make sure your kids are aware of the system you are using and stick only to things you can follow. Do not bargain on rewards. Parenting is not a marketplace – there is no haggling.

Remember that kids are different and need different rewards. **Adapt the reward for the age and character of each child** and do not be tempted to tell "old time stories" of how in the old days, your reward was the shoes you got for Christmas.

Rewards are appropriate regardless of the outcome. If you reward success only, it is a formula to de-motivate. Reward progress and participation.

Privileges are great rewards. You can be very creative with this technique. I gave my kids "permission" to read books and now going to the library is a great reward for them (see my blog post The Book Whisperer). Use them but never abuse them and alternate them so your kids do not get used to them.

Remember the ultimate aim is to **teach your kids to reward themselves**. Do not expect them to do it easily when they are young but to help them develop this ability give them opportunities and choices to reward themselves.

Chapter 9: Emotional Stretch

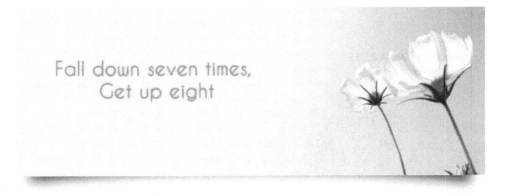

Fall down seven times,
Get up eight

Emotional stretching is a good technique to motivate kids, because it is gradual movement forward. **Explain to your kids how stretches develop character and strength** and encourage them to recognize when they are stretching themselves positively.

It is not about what happens to us but what we do about it. **No matter how small the progress is, as long as the direction is forward, it is a sign of growth.** Learn to appreciate small stretches and highlight them to add up to your child's confidence bowl.

Explain to your kids that doing just a bit every time can take them a long way and all they need to do is focus on the next step, even if they want to climb a high mountain. **Teach your kids to do "just a little bit more"**.

As a parent, appreciate the power of **one more second** and count seconds if you want to monitor the progress.

Children are born with this natural ability to stretch themselves. It reaches a peak at the age of 5 (we call it the Thomas Edison mentality) and starts declining at the age of 11 until its funeral at the age of 16. This is not a natural process. It is caused by grownups inability to stretch themselves and be flexible.

Start early when they already have some of this ability and encourage it and share your stretches with your kids so you can be a good role model of emotional stretch.

Motivation is encouraging stretches. Remember it is painful; this is why it is called stretch. Do not try to do all of them at once. **Even rubber bands have a limit to their ability to stretch**.

If in the process, **you child is "torn"**, it does not mean you have stretched him/her. It means you went too far and will be considered forceful and aggressive, which can't go hand in hand with motivation. Be gentle, chunk it down and if it didn't work, don't blame the child, chunk it down again.

Emotional stretch promotes **self-regulation**. Self-regulation is like a muscle that needs to be constantly stretch in order to grow, though, it is important for the owner of this muscle to control the stretch and not be stretched by force. Self-regulation is essential and will give the kids the best tool to be successful in life though, it is hard to self-regulate on many things at once.

Chapter 10: Inspiration

Inspiration is a gentle form of motivating. **Learning from others** who have "done it" gives kids the necessary belief it is possible. When we teach our kids to learn from others, we plant a GPS in their mind to guide them towards success and happiness.

People can be a great inspiration for all of us. Make stock of all the people you have met in your life and find out how they have supported the person you are today.

Teach your kids "taking" skills and not only with the things you give them. You can be a very inspiring person, but if your kids do not know how to learn from you, the inspiration goes to waste.

We can take inspiration from **all people around us**. They can be people we know closely, people we know a little, or total strangers.

"If you only do what you know you can do, you never do very much"

- Tom Krause

© www.ronitbaras.com

Be positive and aim to say good things about others. Having a positive outlook on life helps "take inspiration" more than seeing faults, judge or criticize. Model giving compliments, expressing appreciation and taking inspiration from others.

Envy can be a source of inspiration – use it! Make sure it does not become judgmental by shifting it to inspiration. This can be done using the 3 shifting questions" *Who is your inspiration?" "What is inspiring about them?"* and help your kids realize what they already have by asking, *"Are you inspiring already?"*

Every character trait you want your kids to have, **start teaching it as early as possible**. It is much harder to start when your kids are already teens (when they need motivation the most).

Share your inspiration list with them to give them ideas and give them legitimization to take inspiration from o people other than mom and dad. Make sure you are not threatened by it.

Help your kids realize what they already have in them that can lead them to where they want to go. Using existing traits is always easier than learning new ones.

Pick the character traits you would like your kids to have and link them to people who possess these traits. Remember, your kids do not have enough life experience to choose the right people to spend time with. It is your responsibility to direct them to the most inspirational people. If you are that person, to make sure your kids will be influenced by you, spend more time with them.

Find books and movies that will transfer the messages you want to give your kids and focus on movies or books with characters that possess the traits you would like your child to have. It is amazing how a trait parents have been trying to pass on to their kids for years can be understood perfectly in just 2 hours of watching one animation movie

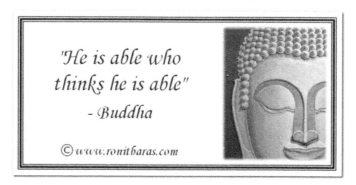

"He is able who thinks he is able"
- Buddha

© www.ronitbaras.com

We are not born with all the traits we need in life, but we can work on developing them. Make sure you understand this; it will minimize your judgment of yourself and your children. Help your kids understand it is a lifelong process and we can be anything we want to be.

Remember the first rules of motivating. It is about what they want not just what you want. Try to find out what character traits they want and compare your child's definition of the traits to your own definition. If you have a conflict, use your child's definition. Why? Because it is the only way to motivate him/her if his/her subconscious thinks he/she is forced, the crew will start the machine guns and you've missed your opportunity to motivate.

Chapter 11: Fear, Fear, go away

Fear is a natural feeling of perceived danger. Remember it does not have to be real at all. If you want to understand it, think of anxiety. It is a fear of something that never happened, something that will be (or not) in the future.

Some parents think fear it is a great motivator, because it makes kids do what the parents want, but in fact, **fear creates only short-term gain, but long-term pain, and the pain lasts even longer**.

Fear is not a healthy method of motivating kids, because it teaches the kids to perceive danger in your words and actions, making you someone they cannot trust. Remember, fear breeds more fear and is a strong inhibitor and makes kids totally paralyzed and not able to make decisions or to develop self-motivation.

Do not confuse procrastination with fear. **Fear is a strong action inhibitor**. Many behaviors that seem unmotivated are often strong reactions to fear.

You need to **discover your kids' fears** in order to help them overcome them. If there are people who make them afraid, encourage them to stay away from those people. Do not abuse this knowledge to gain power and it is your role to **protect them from any other person who does.**

Respect your child's fear of sharing his fears. Make sure you always say, *"I am here if you need me"* at the end of any communication. Always leave the door open to ask for your help.

Never, never, never use fear or threats as a parenting tool if you don't want to lose your kid's trust. Use of fear or threats is a sign of weakness and is a bullying act. It will only "inspire" them to stay away from you to avoid the fear. Remember, bullying parents only raise little victims.

Talk about your fears with your kids. It is not a sign of weakness but a source of inspiration to your kids. It will show them you are human and help legitimize their fears. If you share your way of overcoming this fear, it will inspire them as well.

Help your kids develop healthy ways to deal with their fears. We all have fears. The difference is in how we deal with them. Connect the conquering fears to emotional stretch, growth and development and reward conquering fears. Again, not the end result but the courage to take a risk and face the fear.

Chapter 12: Planning and deadlines

Planning is good for motivation. It helps your kids deal with their fear of the unknown. Many kids seem unmotivated when fear makes them unable to move forward. Planning can help them see options they cannot see otherwise.

Planning is another form of chunking down. It allows children and grownups to overcome the chaos of life and relax. It helps them regain control over their life and the "crew" likes it and cooperates.

Parents with good time skills raise kids with good time skills. Work on your time management skills and master them. Evaluate your current time table to make sure you are not "Stealing" sleep time from yourself. Find your time wasters and get rid of them. Remember, 10 minutes and another 10 minutes adds up.

Collect time management tips and try implementing them one by one. No one is born a time lord, but everyone can become one. Remember, time flies but you are the pilot. You can use the time management **quotes as inspiration**.

Use a calendar to teach planning. Not everyone likes calendars, but you can find something that suits your kids' taste. I used a calendar with 2-year-olds who could not read a word to tell them what the plan of the day was by using pictures and stickers.

Use a **family calendar** to encourage collaboration and consideration between family members. It is simple and cheap.

Deadlines can be sticks or carrots, depending on your kid's personal style. Work your way towards carrots and follow your kids' style. If he/she is performing well, do not force your style on him/her.

Deadlines are only effective as self-motivators. When kids set their own deadlines, they get motivated, but when the deadlines are external, they can inspire fear (fear and motivation cannot go together).

Use **what, where, when, who and how questions** to practice planning. Give kids opportunities to plan a birthday, dinner, trip…. The quality of our life is as good as the quality of our questions.

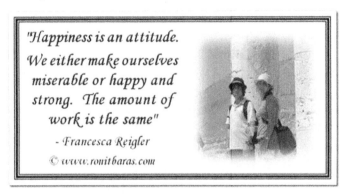

"*Happiness is an attitude. We either make ourselves miserable or happy and strong. The amount of work is the same*"

- *Francesca Reigler*

© *www.ronitbaras.com*

Like the saying **"practice makes perfect"** and the more you let them practice time, the better they will be at managing it. As always, the earlier the better. Any child, from 3 years old can start planning and practice time management. Do not expect them to do things perfectly on the first attempt.

Chapter 13: Promote team work

Teamwork can be a good source of motivation. Performance should be better with kids who are motivated by teamwork. Make sure to study your kids and find out whether they are the type of kids that will enjoy and be motivated by working in a team. Some kids are not, and it is quite OK. Not all kids are the same

Kids who work well in a team can easily **overcome the fear of being alone, shame and ridicule**. They can share the burden of the **responsibility** with others. They ask for more help and take more risks. Though responsibility is important, we can't give it to kids, we must give them the skills to allow them to take it.

Competition can be a good or bad motivator depending on the child, the competitor and the rules of the competition. It is good when team work is involved and not good when the main focus is on the end result.

You can **assess if your kids are too competitive** if they make superior comments, blames others for challenges and difficulties and talk lots about being fair losing or winning. It usually means they are very frustrated kids.

Overly competitive kids should not be encouraged to use this technique as a motivator. Those kids are usually motivated by the fear of failure. Perfectionists are harder to deal with than unmotivated kids.

If your kids are too competitive, **consider your attitude**. Kids are mirrors. Sometimes we do not pay attention, but our desire for them to succeed and excel can give messages of competitiveness.

If you want competition to work to your advantage, **emphasize the process and not the end result**. When kids learn that the process has a lot more to offer than the end result, they "enjoy the ride" and are less frustrated by things not going exactly as they expect.

Even when you use the competition for motivating, **focus on teamwork**. Competition as a team and not against others in the team can bring the morale up.

In the argument between nature and nurture, the teamwork skill is probably a mix of the two. If your kids were lucky to win the lottery of their genetic disposition and have those skills naturally, lucky them! Lucky you! If not, every skill can be developed.

Chapter 14: Permission to motivate

Love and intention are not enough to make you a successful motivator. It is not enough for you to want to help. Your kids need to want your help.

When you want to motivate your kids effectively, **get their permission first!** Otherwise, your advice may be considered an invasion. **Permission is a non-verbal contract between the giver and receiver.**

Getting permission from your kids will make sure the motivation to succeed (the ownership of success) is in your kids' hands. Permission is a sign of good communication between kids and parents. Nagging is a sign the relationship is missing respect. Think about it as an invasion or a boomerang.

If parents try to motivate **without permission, kids may treat it as nagging or forcing and reject the help regardless of how much they need it**. It starts a cycle of nagging that triggers a fear of nagging which make the parent nag even more and sabotages the relationship.

To understand your parents' love you must raise children yourself

— Chinese Proverb

Nagging is a form of bullying. The nagger puts pressure on the nagged to do something the naggers wants. It usually involves shame, fear, judgment, humiliation, guilt, ridicule, sarcasm and all those things create fear. <u>**Motivation cannot happen in the presence of fear**</u>.

Supported and encouraged kids blossom while nagged kids misbehave, lie, hide and develop low self-esteem. Support becomes nagging when you rate what is important to you higher than what is important to your child. Nagging de-motivates kids. Read this over and over again. I know it is hard to accept this, but according to Choice Theory, nagging is one of the reasons for many relationship breakdowns, because it involves criticism in disguise.

Nagging parents raise nagging kids. Check your own nagging history **who nagged you and how do you nag, on what topics and why**? Find patterns and correlations between you and your own naggers. It will help you understand the dynamic between you and your own kids.

Do not be tempted to be the cow who wants to feed more than the calf wants to drink. Seek permission! **Do not force your help: ask the child in a sincere tone of voice (without sarcasm, please!)** *"Do you need help?" "How can I help?" "What would you like me to do when…?" "How do you suggest I react when…?"* If you want to understand how important the tone of the voice is, ask those questions with sarcasm and then with the real desire to know the answer and notice that one of them is aggressive and the other is caring.

When asking permission, *take into consideration that your child may say "no"*. Your reaction to your kids' acceptance or refusal to get help will build or destroy the trust you kids has in you. You don't want them to think you will help them only if they do what you want them to do. This is not motivation. It is teaching "obedience" and is very forceful.

Kids will approve your offer to help or not based on the quality of the relationship with their parents. They will differentiate between mom and dad depending on their individual relationship with them. They will approve your suggestions in some areas **and not others**. When they are afraid of nagging, when they are worried, they will be considered weak, when they don't want your help, or if they feel that asking permission is a way to manipulate them, they will refuse your offer.

Asking permission to help or motivate kids is a test every parent experience. Sometimes kids will say "no" to our offers to help and support them and "flashing" with our intentions and love won't work. No matter how hard it is to get a "no" for a request to help, **always leave the door open**. Tell them you will be there for them to help and support them and that you respect their choices even if you disagree with them. If you leave the door open, it'll be much easier for them to use it when they are in trouble.

Chapter 15: Gentle reminders

When things are very hard, kids (and grownups) tend to **give up as a natural mechanism to handle disappointment or failure.** Don't take it too hard. You can help your child by developing his/her **"Can do" attitude.** It is a good way to make sure your motivation tools will be sustainable.

"Can do" parents raise "can do" kids. It is as easy as just **being a role model**. Find the things you can inspire your kids to do. **Inspiration is a very gentle and effective motivating strategy**. If you can't be inspiration, find someone who can.

After you have your kids' permission, consider **gentle reminders** as an easy and effective way to motivate them without being considered a nagger.

Gentle reminders can sometimes be used even when your kids **do not give you permission to help them** (note I wrote "gentle"). The opposite of gentleness is aggressiveness. Again, you cannot force kids to accept help.

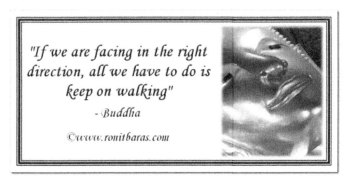

"If we are facing in the right direction, all we have to do is keep on walking"
- Buddha

©www.ronitbaras.com

Gentle reminders need to be positive. Sarcastic reminders are not positive. Stay away from sarcasm if you want to motivate your kids. Don't use sarcasm or negative statements, don't use name-calling and don't be a dark prophet. It triggers fear. Keep in mind you are helping them for their sake and not yours.

Share your own inspiration and learning experiences. They are fantastic motivators. Sharing your own experience does not require asking permission. Your kids can learn lots about you from the sentences you repeatedly use.

Use questions as reminders. Focus on gentle. Do it in a subtle way so they won't hear any judgment or sarcasm in your tone of voice. If they are not sarcastic, they will just be reminders.

Offer to help as a gentle reminder.

When you remind your kids to do something, it is for him/her, not for you. Keep in mind that **your kids' feelings are the main issue here and not yours.** You are there to help them. You remind them to do something they want, not something you want.

Quotes can be guidelines to use to navigate life. They are excellent gentle reminders. Everything we repeat over and over again functions as a quote. It is true for good statements and true for very negative, cruel, sad, disappointing statements. Watch your words and consider how your kids will quote you when they grow older.

Quotes can be found in your repeated sentences, statements/quotes of others, movies, books, politicians, celebrities, religious leaders, proverbs, philosophers. There are millions of them. Make your own collection.

You can **find quotes in sentences you use, people you know, movies, books and quote sites.** They don't have to be famous people in order to quote them. They have to be short, easy to remember and to the point.

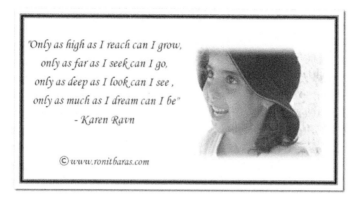

"Only as high as I reach can I grow,
only as far as I seek can I go,
only as deep as I look can I see,
only as much as I dream can I be"
- Karen Ravn

© www.ronitbaras.com

Match the quotes to your kids' age and language level. Make sure they are clear, positive and not sarcastic.

Sometimes **when the source of the sentence is not the parent, it has a greater influence,** especially when there is a conflict between the parent and the child. It is a very gentle way of backing up what you repeatedly think (and can't say)

Quotes inspire self-motivating ideas that will later become part of who your kids are. They will be reflected in their behaviors and their attitude towards the world around them.

Chapter 16: Affirmation for self-motivation

Affirmations are the thoughts and beliefs we have that help us navigate through life. You can use them to encourage your kids to move forward. Remember, moving forward towards something they want is called motivation.

The good thing about affirmations is **that your kids can use them when you are not around** and long after they have left home.

Your kid's mind is a garden and you are the gardeners. Things you say and do function as seeds. The seeds will grow either to be happy flowers or poisonous fears. Watch your actions and words.

It is easier to plant seeds of love than to uproot poison plants, but uprooting is not impossible. Start early!

Self-talk/self-chatter is a self-preserving function that is supposed to help us make choices and decisions. It either warns us or encourages us to do things. Positive self-talk uses happy encouraging, courageous, self-esteem boosting affirmations. Negative self-talk uses scary, fearful, sad, worried, debilitating and stressful affirmations.

Most of the affirmations we have are beliefs collected throughout our childhood when we were inexperienced and dependent on our parents and those who were close to us. **Don't blame kids for having negative affirmations, help them change them.**

The **best two ways to instill affirmations is to model or verbalize them.** They work best if they come together when you repeat your words and your actions are consistent with your words. Make sure they do not contradict each other. Otherwise, your child will not trust you to be a credible source of affirmations.

Make a conscious choice to evaluate your own affirmations and be reflective and honest with yourself. If you have affirmations you don't like, you don't have to keep them just because they have been there for years.

Motivating your kids is like giving them a fish, while teaching them to motivate themselves is like teaching them to fish using a fishing net. **It may take longer to knit a fishing net, but it will guarantee they will need less energy later**. Repeat and model over and over again and if you feel it takes too long and wonder how long it will take, here is a rule for you. If they can motivate themselves, you're done, if not, you need to keep on doing it until they do.

Chapter 17: External influences and sustainability

Find your kids' influencers and deal with de-motivators. Parenting is easier when you know the obstacles to transferring your values.

Find out if your kids think about their influencers the same way you do. You will be surprised to find that from some influencers you consider bad for your kids, they learn "how not to behave", which is a good thing.

Talk to your kids about the people who influence their life. Kids are just young and lack experience and long-term perspective. Highlight your differences in values and talk to them about that influence.

Counter de-motivation with encouragement and positivity motivating ideas and thoughts and never badmouth others.

Find your own influencers and de motivators. It will help you assess your values and be a better role model. Be honest!

When you find out your motivating techniques are working, **focus on self-motivation** to make sure it will continue long after yours stops. Your motivation is sustainable when your kids can motivate themselves through self-care, self-appreciation and self-pride.

Kids and adults confuse pride with bragging, boasting and being "full of yourself". Teach your kids the difference between arrogance and pride and encourage them to be proud of themselves. Share achievements, receive compliments and allow them to do the same.

Ceremonies of pride done in a group are very successful and motivating when done in the family. It gives permission to everyone to fill up their own confidence bowl. Any family gathering is a good opportunity to play the self-appreciation game and it does not take long for kids to start enjoying it.

How long will you have to motivate your kids? **As long as you are alive.**

When will you know you have succeeded? When your kids are proud of themselves and express it. When they give themselves the permission to motivate themselves and **when you hear the sentence** *"I am proud of me"*

"Believe you can and you're half way there"
- Theodore Roosevelt

© www.ronitbaras.com

Our kids reflect us and when they say *"I am proud of myself"* they reflect the pride we have in ourselves for motivating them to be the best they can be, happy, smart, courageous, friendly, healthy, loving, kind, trustworthy, appreciative, respectful, forgiving, faithful and happy.

When your motivation techniques become sustainable, it is time for you to fill up your confidence bowl, celebrate and be proud for your own success.

Imagine yourself standing on the graduation stage, proud as a peacock as you have mastered the art of motivating your kids.

Happy and easy motivating,
Ronit

OTHER BOOKS BY RONIT BARAS

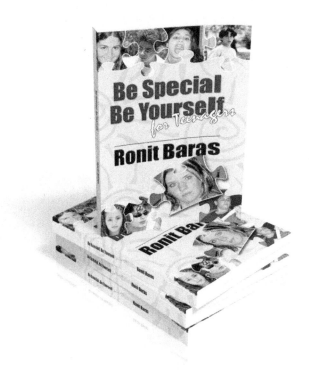

Be Special, Be Yourself for Teenagers is a collection of 8 short stories for teens, dealing with the conflict between the desire to be unique and the desire to be loved and accepted.

Whether they are different, from the future, from a different country or have unusual circumstances, the characters of Be Special, Be Yourself, teenagers and adults, struggle with giving up their significance to gain love.

They wrestle with body image, social acceptance, family relationships, school, diversity and inclusion. Invariable, it's their attitude that determines their fate.

OTHER BOOKS BY RONIT BARAS

Living an ordinary life, journalist Jay Banks gets the chance of a lifetime to interview the dying world-famous author Katherine Johnson. In her wildest dreams, Jay could not predict the unusual encounter with Katherine Johnson would shake her and make her question every important aspect of her life. Suddenly, every action, feeling, relationship and choice is cast in doubt…

Jay's story offers every reader, young and old, a fresh and powerful way to examine the most important parts of life and shift from ordinary existence to fascinating and exciting living.

Joining Jay Banks, as she goes through pain and awakening on her journey of liberation, allows readers to take an important step forward towards their own personal freedom.

OTHER BOOKS BY RONIT BARAS

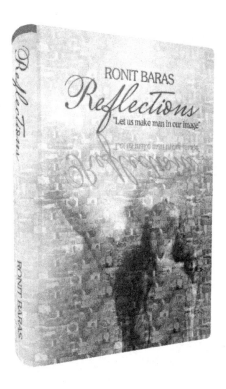

A story of realization, where fantasy and reality, life and death, pain and pleasure are woven together. It peels back the layers of our beliefs about love, happiness, birth, death, friendship, money, power, parenting, family and spirituality and reveals to us the power within.

After 16-year-old Ella decides that life is not worth living, she meets Sam, a mysterious old man, who starts her on a new life of discovery. He guides her through world travels, excitement and pain, teaching her about the ultimate divine power.

Who is Sam? Imaginary friend? Guardian angel? God?

OTHER BOOKS BY RONIT BARAS

In his life, Sam Brahms tried desperately to instill in his children and convince his wife to value the important things in life, but he failed. His family members drifted apart with bitterness and resentment in their hearts.

When he died and left a will, to be read a month later, his family didn't know their world would turn upside down. In moments of grief and uncertainty, his ex-wife, his three children and his lawyer are torn between greed and the desire to honor his last wish. They face their biggest fears and question what they value most.

Can Sam's will bring his divided family together or make them drift even further apart? What kind of a legacy will he leave behind him? Will Sam Brahms succeed in death to do what he couldn't do in life?

Made in the USA
Coppell, TX
20 March 2022

75279922R00157